Teaching GCSE History

Teaching GCSE History

Martin Booth, Christopher Culpin and Henry Macintosh

HODDER AND STOUGHTON
LONDON SYDNEY AUCKLAND TORONTO

ISBN 0 340 40951 7

First published 1987

Copyright © 1987 Martin Booth, Christopher Culpin and Henry Macintosh

All rights reserved. No part of this publication may be reproduced or transmitted in any form or by any means, electronically or mechanically, including photocopying, recording or any information storage or retrieval system, without either the prior permission in writing from the publisher or a licence, permitting restricted copying, issued by the Copyright Licensing Agency, 7 Ridgmont Street, London WC1E 7AA.

Typeset by Tradespools Ltd, Frome, Somerset
Printed and bound in Great Britain for
Hodder and Stoughton Educational,
a division of Hodder and Stoughton Ltd,
Mill Road, Dunton Green, Sevenoaks, Kent,
by The Eastern Press Ltd, London and Reading

Contents

Acknowledgments	vi
Introduction	7
1 The national criteria	9
2 Teaching GCSE history	20
3 Assessment in GCSE history	53
Appendix A: Coursework Analysis Instrument	81
Appendix B: Examining Groups for GCSE	85
Selected bibliography	88

Acknowledgments

The authors and publishers would like to thank the following for permission to reproduce material in this book:
The Controller of Her Majesty's Stationery Office for the extracts from *The National Criteria – History* on pp. 12, 14, 17, and 18 and the extract from *The National Criteria – General Criteria* on pp. 85–6; The Salisbury and South Wiltshire Museum for the illustration 1(a) on p. 21; Leicht Furniture Ltd (Orpington) for the photograph 1(b) on p. 21; BBC Hulton Picture Library for the photographs/illustrations on pp. 29, 30, 32 and 44; *The Daily Telegraph* for the extract and illustration on p. 33; The Imperial War Museum for the illustration on p. 34; The Institute of Agricultural History and Museum of English Rural Life, University of Reading for the photograph on p. 37; Popperfoto for the illustration on p. 41; *Punch* magazine for the illustration on p. 39; The Southern Examining Group for the extracts on pp. 60, 63, 66, 69 and 81–4; The Northern Examining Association for the extract on p. 66; The London and East Anglian Group for the extract on p. 60; The Midland Examining Group for the extracts on pp. 66, 68 and 69; The Northern Ireland Schools Examination Council for the extract on p. 61; The Welsh Joint Education Committee for the extracts on pp. 67 and 69; Collins for permission to use material from *Making History* (1984) and *Making British History* (1987), both by Christopher Culpin, in Chapter 2.

Introduction

History teachers embarking on the teaching of GCSE courses may well have three interrelated questions in mind: To what extent does the examination break new ground? What changes will I have to make to my teaching methods? How can I most effectively translate the aims and objectives of the national criteria into classroom teaching and assessment strategies? It is the purpose of this book to try to answer these questions.

There are three main chapters. The first sets the scene by examining the national and draft grade criteria for history and looking critically at the aims and assessment objectives they lay down. Reference is also made to the general criteria to which all syllabuses must also conform. The second chapter then looks at the history criteria in terms of classroom teaching. In particular two main areas will be explored: teaching for conceptual and empathetic understanding and the use of a wide variety of source materials in the classroom. The organisation of coursework will also be examined. This chapter is largely based on practical teaching examples which have been tested in the classroom. In the third chapter the implications of the criteria for assessment are examined. What is the range of assessment instruments available and how valid and reliable are they? Is it possible to differentiate between the performance of the least able and the most able by asking the same questions? How can the responses of candidates to such questions be marked? And how can we organise and assess coursework, which is now mandatory?

The focus of the book, therefore, is tightly on the history national criteria and the ways in which they can be implemented. The broader issues of the place of history within a core curriculum or the role it could play in a modular structure are not examined; nor is there discussion of the resources implications of teaching and assessing GCSE history. These are of course matters of crucial importance, and history teachers need to be alert to the debate and continue to argue for the central place of history in the curriculum as well as for the additional resources necessary; space precludes their consideration in this book.

1 The National Criteria

THE ROLE OF NATIONAL AND DRAFT GRADE CRITERIA FOR HISTORY

The national and general criteria give muscle to the General Certificate of Secondary Education examination structure, the national system for assessment in England, Wales and Northern Ireland which replaced the GCE O level and CSE examinations. The subject–specific criteria aim to reflect the best of teaching and assessment; they provide a national framework for the 14–16 curriculum. It is these national and general criteria which the four examining groups – Northern Examining Association, Midland Examining Group, London and East Anglian Group, Southern Examining Group – and the Welsh Joint Education Committee and the Northern Ireland Schools Examinations Council have to take as the blueprint for all their syllabuses and examinations. The draft grade criteria for ten subjects appeared in 1985 and are an amplification and refinement of the assessment objectives and grade descriptions. It is intended that they should be added to the national criteria at a later stage.

The history national criteria provide a statement about the nature of the subject to be taught and examined, the course aims and assessment objectives. Content in relation to assessment objectives is discussed and techniques of assessment considered. An indication of levels of attainment at grades F and C is given. These criteria were not drawn out of a hat by the working party charged with their drafting; they are the product of extensive consultation with history teachers, the Historical Association, HMI, the examining groups, users of the examinations, the Secondary Examinations Council and the Government. Above all, the criteria reflect many years of debate and development about the teaching and learning of history. At the heart of this has been the increasing dissatisfaction with the Gradgrind approach to history teaching and a growing emphasis on the methods and concepts of the historian, the sources he or she uses and the need to see history as a debate based on evidence.

The national and draft grade criteria for history bring together developments in the teaching and assessment of the subject which have been long in the making. To this extent, history GCSE is not breaking new ground; it is an amalgam of what many would see as the best of history teaching. Yet the GCSE examination system, of which the national and general criteria are arguably the most crucial part, is something new. First, England, Wales and Northern Ireland now have national criteria for twenty subjects in the curriculum (plus the general criteria), frameworks to which all new examination syllabuses which have replaced the GCE O level and CSE examinations must now conform. This gives a degree of standardisation and comparability between examining groups and boards, and within subject areas, which we have not had until now. We have agreed definitions of these subjects, agreed aims and assessment objectives; history, whether taken in schools in Cumbria or Cornwall, County Down or Cambridgeshire, is recognisably the same thing.

Secondly, the criteria in all the subjects stress that skills and conceptual understanding are as important as content, that pupils must be inducted into the process by which knowledge in the subject area is gained. So assessment will be concerned not merely with information learned but with reasoning and enquiry skills; a range of assessment instruments and techniques will be employed to measure pupil achievement. In particular, nearly all subjects now require pupils to undertake coursework; in history a minimum of 20 per cent of the total marks are being given for this.

CRITERION REFERENCING

It is, however, the issue of criterion referencing which most clearly marks the GCSE examination system as something different in kind from the old GCE and CSE examinations. GCE and CSE were norm-referenced examinations. That is, they were concerned with global scores, rank orders and the distributions of candidates over the normal curve of distribution. If for example, a candidate had received a grade A for GCE O level history with board X, all we would have known about his performance was that his score probably came in the top 10 per cent of the group of candidates who took that particular examination. We would have known little about his actual achievement – what he knew, or could do or understand, or indeed how his performance compared with a candidate who got an O level history grade A from board Y.

With criterion-referenced examinations, however, a candidate's performance is judged against clear-cut criteria. Obvious examples of examinations referenced to criteria are the car-driving test or the Associated Board for the Royal School of Music's practical examinations. Note two things about these examples. First, the elements of 'car-driving' or 'practical musicianship' are clearly defined. To be a competent car-driver you must be able to do a three-point turn, a hill start, an emergency stop and so on; to be judged a competent musician (at whatever grade level) you must undertake a sight reading and aural test, play a number of set pieces which you have prepared, and perform certain scales and arpeggios. Secondly, the level of what constitutes competence or mastery in each of these elements is clearly defined. You must do the hill start without letting the car roll back or the engine stall; you must make no more than three mistakes in the sight reading test.

GRADE DESCRIPTIONS AND CRITERIA

Now car-driving or practical musicianship may seem a far cry from history but it is precisely this criteria-referencing exercise which has been attempted for subjects within the GCSE examination. The published national criteria are the first stage in this. These give definitions of the subjects, the aims which must underwrite the teaching and the assessment objectives which will be the concern of the evaluation techniques. The grade criteria, which at the time of writing are in draft form for ten subjects only, are expected to be grafted on to the national criteria at a later date. The grade criteria will replace the grade descriptions and provide statements of the mastery to be achieved at (provisionally) four levels of competence for each of the assessment objectives. We may therefore eventually have a matrix against which a candidate's performance can be compared and reported on. After the examination we will know what the candidate has positively achieved in history, what he or she knows, understands and can do.

GCSE certificates in future may thus show not only the overall grade awarded for a particular subject on the seven-point A–G scale, with the old GCE boards taking responsibility for grades A–C, but also a breakdown of how that grade was achieved in terms of performance in particular assessment areas. For example, in history the draft grade criteria at the moment point to three main assessment areas (or 'domains', as they are termed): historical knowledge and understanding (an area encompassing the conceptual and empathetic understanding of history teaching); historical enquiry (an area covering the enquiry skills of project work or coursework); historical reasoning (an area dealing with the intellectual skills required when using historical source materials). A certificate could show candidate X's overall performance in history as, for example, grade C (i.e. equivalent to the old GCE grade C or CSE grade 1) but also record the levels of mastery achieved in each of the three areas indicated above. It should be said, however, that doubts are being expressed as to how far such a general matrix and reporting scheme would be workable in practice.

Practical Implications

The full implementation of grade criteria is yet to come; for the moment teachers will be concerned with the national criteria and their implications for teaching and assessment. In section 1 'General' (Fig. 1) and section 2 'Aims' (Fig. 2) the *National Criteria – History* state that the subject has a unique contribution to make to the curriculum, particularly as regards the understanding of the development of social and cultural values. No other subject is concerned with the recreation of mankind's past. Historical knowledge, however, must be regarded as debatable and provisional, though it will be supported by a range of evidence. The methodology of historians, the sources they use and the concepts (for example, cause and consequence, con-

> **General**
>
> 1.1 There are two broad avenues of approach in History teaching, differing in the emphasis placed on the relative importance of "content" and "skills" in the study of the subject. The criteria apply to the subject as a whole and provide for these different approaches.
>
> 1.2 History is primarily concerned with re-creating mankind's past. Statements are made which are provisional yet which are derived from evidence. A range of concepts is employed, many of which are shared with other disciplines. There are, however, concepts such as continuity and change which are of particular concern to the study of History. It is in the combination of these elements that History makes its particular contribution to the curriculum.

▲ *Fig. 1*

> **Aims**
>
> The aims of a History course are
>
> 2.1 to stimulate interest in and enthusiasm for the study of the past;
>
> 2.2 to promote the acquisition of knowledge and understanding of human activity in the past, linking it, as appropriate, with the present;
>
> 2.3 to ensure that candidates' knowledge is rooted in an understanding of the nature and the use of historical evidence;
>
> 2.4 to help pupils, particularly in courses on British History, towards an understanding of the development over time of social and cultural values;
>
> 2.5 to promote an understanding of the nature of cause and consequence, continuity and change, similarity and difference;
>
> 2.6 to develop essential study skills such as the ability to locate and extract information from primary and secondary sources; to detect bias; to analyse this information and to construct a logical argument (usually through the medium of writing);
>
> 2.7 to provide a sound basis for further study and the pursuit of personal interest.

▶ *Fig. 2*

tinuity and change, similarity and difference) must therefore play as large a part in the teaching of history as content. What then specifically will GCSE history be concerned with assessing? Section 3 of the *Criteria* spells out the Assessment Objectives.

ASSESSMENT OBJECTIVES

Historical Knowledge and Understanding

> **Assessment Objectives**
>
> All candidates will be expected
>
> 3.1 to recall, evaluate and select knowledge relevant to the context and to deploy it in a clear and coherent form;
>
> 3.2 to make use of and understand the concepts of cause and consequence, continuity and change, similarity and difference;
>
> 3.3 to show an ability to look at events and issues from the perspective of people in the past;

▲ *Fig. 3*

The first three objectives (Fig. 3) are concerned with the knowledge and understanding which, after all, are the aim or purpose of studying history. Now the criteria make it clear that historical knowledge only becomes understanding if it is used, shaped or deployed in some way. Information must therefore be recalled or selected to serve some particular purpose: for example, a description could be required, or a narrative of events.

Often historians use a concept or pair of concepts to shape their knowledge. For example, the concept of causation is one which is frequently used; we select information to explain the causes of a particular event, distinguishing between the long-term and the immediate, the contingent and the deliberate. We also often employ the concepts of similarity and difference, continuity and change, to shape our information: we compare and contrast, for example, a picture of a cottage industry with one of an early nineteenth-century factory, or a photograph of the High Street in 1900 with one of the present. These are key methodological concepts in history and will shape and structure our information, whatever period or topic we study.

However, we also use what can be termed substantive concepts, many of which may be particular to that part of history we are studying. For example, the concept of nationalism or imperialism may well be of crucial importance in a study of nineteenth-century Europe, or fascism in a study of twentieth-century Italy. Concepts, then, serve as catalysts for knowledge: they help to make sense of the past by giving it structure and coherence. They raise historical knowledge from the level of 'one damn thing after another' to that of historical understanding – a past, that is, that makes sense.

Now, all this could be interpreted as encouraging the old-style essay – the forty minute slog in answer to the set question such as 'Discuss the causes of ...' In fact, both the national and general criteria (as well as the assessment procedures they encourage) make it clear that 'fitness for the purpose' is the key. There will be times when a sustained piece of writing is required, and others when shorter, pithier statements will suffice. More than this, it is by no means an essential requirement that historical understanding is displayed in written form. For example, oral presentations could be used; so too could slide–tape sequences or role-play exercises.

Empathy

There is another aspect to this historical understanding, an aspect which the criteria emphasise in Assessment Objective 3.3: historical empathy. The criteria in fact do not use the word; the objective states that candidates will be expected 'to show an ability to look at events and issues from the perspective of people in the past'. Empathy is the word which sums this up. It is a notoriously difficult objective to teach, mainly because we are often unsure as to what it is we are trying to achieve. Only too often our empathy lessons end up with exhortations to the pupils to imagine what it was like to be a medieval peasant toiling away in the open field system, or a child miner in the nineteenth century; our pupils respond either with wild and unhistorical flights of fancy or a dull, stilted account culled from the textbook. Empathy in history certainly demands imagination, but it is an imagination strictly controlled by the context and the evidence. In essence, empathy is the attempt to get to grips with the strangeness of the past. Why was it, for example, that medieval people continued to be touched for the king's evil in spite of the fact that the majority would never be cured? Why weren't Elizabethan people outraged by the government's use of torture? Why were so many Americans in the 1950s taken in by the accusations of Senator McCarthy? Empathy is therefore at the heart of historical understanding; increasingly, teachers and examiners are realising that it is best approached by tackling a problem and carefully structuring the learning materials. We

Use of Source Material

Comprehension and interpretation

> 3.4 to show the skills necessary to study a wide variety of historical evidence which should include both primary and secondary written sources, statistical and visual material, artefacts, text books and orally transmitted information
>
> 3.4.1 by comprehending and extracting information from it;
>
> 3.4.2 by interpreting and evaluating it — distinguishing between fact, opinion and judgement; pointing to deficiencies in the material as evidence, such as gaps and inconsistencies; detecting bias;
>
> 3.4.3 by comparing various types of historical evidence and reaching conclusions based on this comparison.

▲ *Fig. 4*

have indeed moved a long way from the 'imagine you are a Red guard' approach.

Narratives, descriptions, conceptual and empathetic understanding, therefore, are the products of our study. The ways in which we achieve this knowledge and understanding are dealt with in Assessment Objective 3.4 (Fig. 4) which is concerned with the skills necessary to study a wide range of historical source material.

Virtually anything can be a source to the historian – anything, that is, from graffiti to a rusty nail, a fragment of a pot to a half-remembered story. We may not as teachers often turn to such sources, preferring instead the eyewitness account, the ambassador's telling letter or the vivid photograph; and there will be few teachers who have not at some time or other enlivened their lessons with an account of, say, the execution of Mary Queen of Scots or the Battle of Agincourt. Many of us, too, may have asked our pupils to get information about an event by using a particular piece of source material. Now, these are perfectly legitimate ways of using source materials, but the criteria make it clear that we must go much further than this. We must first of all understand the crucial distinction between a source and evidence. A source only becomes evidence when it is capable of serving some particular purpose, of answering a particular question that we may put to it.

The distinction is nicely made in an episode in the Conan Doyle story of 'The Adventure of the Blue Carbuncle'. Peterson, the commissionaire of Holmes's block of flats, is walking home in the small hours of Christmas morning. Ahead of him he sees a man, wearing a bowler hat and carrying over his shoulder a white goose, no doubt destined for the table later that day. Suddenly out of the shadows a knot of toughs set on the man carrying the goose. Peterson rushes to his defence and beats off the attackers. They disappear into the gloom; but so, to Peterson's surprise, does the man with the white goose. And, as he rushes off, he drops the goose and the bowler hat slips from his head. Peterson takes both goose and hat to Sherlock Holmes to see if he can make anything of the incident. Holmes carefully examines the bowler and, in response to Watson's scepticism ('What can you gather from this battered old felt?'), challenges the doctor by saying 'Here is my lens. You know my methods. What can you gather yourself as to the individuality of the man who has worn this article?' But to Watson the hat is nothing but a dusty, battered object; it can offer no evidence about the man who wore it. Holmes, on the other hand, has turned the source into evidence by asking questions, by looking for the clues. He states confidently that the man who wore the hat was highly intellectual, was once fairly well-to-do but had fallen on hard times and perhaps taken to the bottle, led a sedentary life, going out but little, and was out of condition. The house he lived in almost certainly did not have gas. Moreover, he was middle-aged, had recently visited the barber, had grey hair and wore hair cream. What was more, he was married to a wife who no longer loved him.

The evidence Holmes deduced from the hat is, of course, for the most part somewhat far-fetched. The man must be intelligent because the hat is so large; the hat was an expensive make but was three years old – the man can now no longer afford to replace it; he must be in poor health because the inner band is drenched with sweat; the hair cream can be smelt and the grey hair seen; surely no wife who loved her husband would allow him out in an unbrushed hat – and so on. The point, however, about the distinction between a source and evidence can be well made through the story, though we must be careful not to press the analogy between an historian and a detective too far; pupils can then be encouraged to look at sources and to ask what these could be evidence for. For example, the famous First World War recruiting poster depicting Kitchener ('Your country needs YOU') could be used as evidence of the government's propaganda techniques; the Rowlandson cartoon which followed the introduction of smallpox vaccination showing cows emerging from various parts of the treated people's bodies could be taken as evidence of late-eighteenth-century attitudes towards Jenner's work. The comprehension and interpretation of the source will then follow; pupils must try to get to grips with the material, to understand it and to offer some sort of an interpretation. This will involve attempting to put the source into its historical context – understanding, for example, that the excessively obsequious language of a letter is merely the convention of the time and not the work of an odious creep. Interpretation may also be concerned with the translation of a source from one form to another. For example, presented with a graph of birth and death rates from 1750 to the present, pupils should be able to explain the information it conveys and assess its significance; looking at an aerial photograph of a deserted medieval village, they should be able to describe its main features.

Reliability and bias

Comprehension and interpretation lead on to a consideration of the reliability and bias of a source. We talk about a reliable witness and mean someone who is accurate and does not distort the truth. A source can in fact be highly reliable in the sense that the information it contains is accurate, but biased in the sense that the information has been selected to give a particular slant or viewpoint. Such bias, of course, can range from the deliberate intention to distort to an unconsciously expressed viewpoint. Pupils must therefore be encouraged to ask of a written source: Who wrote it and for what purpose? When did he or she write it? Had the writer a particular axe to grind? Was he or she present at the events described? Is the information reliable? How can we check? A similar set of questions could be asked of pictorial sources or orally transmitted information. Artefacts can also be questioned for their purpose and authenticity; so can buildings (is the ruined castle behind the eighteenth-century house really what it purports to be? For what reason was it built?). Indeed, virtually any source can distort or misrepresent, and pupils must constantly be evaluating it; in the words of the criteria, 'distinguishing between fact, opinion and judgment; pointing to deficiencies in the material as evidence, such as gaps and inconsistencies, detecting bias'.

Reaching a conclusion

The final stage will be the attempt to reach some sort of conclusion based on the evidence extracted from the source. Sometimes, of course, our conclusion must be 'not proven because of insufficient evidence'; often we make our conclusion with reference to other sources and information. For example, when examining a photograph of poor Edwardian children a pupil might conclude that the children came from poor families, supporting this assertion not only by reference to the appearance of the children, their ragged clothing and lack of footwear, but also to reports from school medical officers and Charles Booth's survey of the London poor.

Primary and secondary sources

In dealing with historical source material we have made no reference so far to the distinction between primary and secondary sources; yet Assessment Objective 3.4 makes it clear that pupils must view secondary material as well as primary as a source of evidence. At first sight, the distinction seems easy. A primary source is the raw material or building block of the historian – the document, picture or artefact from the period studied; the secondary source is the finished product, for example, the account written by the historian which is based on the evidence extracted from the primary sources. Thus the Act of Supremacy 1534 is a primary source; G.R. Elton's *England under the Tudors* (1955) is a secondary source based on evidence derived from primary sources such as the Act of Supremacy.

However, the distinction is often not nearly so clear-cut. Is Clarendon's *The History of the Rebellion* (which appeared in the late seventeenth century) a secondary or primary source? It depends what use we want to make of it. If we are concerned with contemporary attitudes to the English Civil Wars, we might well consider it to be a primary source; if, on the other hand, we take it as one interpretation of the events, then we would be using it as a secondary source. Secondary sources, indeed, must be subjected to the same scrutiny as primary: we need to ask who wrote it, for what purpose, when; has the author based his or her account on the work of other historians, or has he or she gone back to the primary sources; how reliable or biased is the work? Pupils can find it an interesting and sometimes startling exercise to compare a number of different textbook accounts of the same event. What omissions, contrasts, differences and similarities can they note?

CONTENT

The Assessment Objectives in section 3 of the criteria set out the immediate teaching agenda; we next deal with the issue of content and its relationship with these objectives. Here the criteria are open-ended (Fig. 5). There is no attempt to stipulate a minimum core of content. All that is laid down is that each of the examining groups must offer 'at least one syllabus which helps pupils towards an understanding of the intellectual, cultural, technological and political growth of the United Kingdom and of the effects of these developments on the lives of its citizens'; otherwise all that is required is that syllabuses must meet certain broad criteria. They must be of sufficient length, range and depth to enable the assessment objectives to be taught effectively. It would, for example, be difficult to reach an understanding of change and continuity if the syllabus consisted of a study in depth of, say, the government of Lord Liverpool, 1812–27; it might be hard to develop empathetic understanding if the syllabus concentrated on a line-of-development study of transport from earliest times to the present; it might not be easy to find time for much source-based work if the syllabus was concerned with giving an outline understanding of the history of the world from prehistory to the present.

The criteria also state that syllabuses must deal with key issues and be historically coherent and balanced. Such criteria give considerable latitude. There are four examples of syllabuses given in the *Criteria* which exemplify this. They range from a modern world history syllabus, 1919 to the present, to the Schools Project discontinuous pattern – a line of development (say medicine), a study in depth (say Britain 1815–51), a modern world study (say the Arab-Israeli conflict) and a local study. The criteria of length, range and key issues are all self-evidently met by both syllabuses. The modern world syllabus has coherence through its chronological framework; coherence is provided for the Schools Project by the emphasis in all parts of the syllabus on the nature and use of evidence.

Content and its Relationship with Assessment Objectives

4.1 It is in the professional tradition of the discipline and inherent in its nature that candidates should be able to study History in its varied contexts. This variety is apparent in the CSE and GCE O-Level History syllabuses which were analysed. The Examining Groups should, therefore, provide a wide range of options to give freedom to innovate and to reflect local interests. It is therefore not desirable to stipulate a minimum core of content.

Each GCSE Examining Group must offer at least one syllabus which helps pupils towards an understanding of the intellectual, cultural, technological and political growth of the United Kingdom and of the effects of these developments on the lives of its citizens.

4.2 For the above reasons these criteria have been couched in terms of aims and assessment objectives rather than of content. Such aims and assessment objectives in any GCSE History course should be the common ground in syllabuses and will help in the achievement of comparable performance standards in the award of grades.

4.3 Nevertheless, aims and objectives clearly have important implications for determining course content. In order to allow the assessment objectives to be realised, syllabuses must satisfy the following criteria:

    4.3.1   they must be of sufficient length, range and depth;

    4.3.2   they must deal with key issues;

    4.3.3   they must be historically coherent and balanced.

    NOTE: Syllabus content should be given in some detail and not merely consist of starting and terminal dates. Syllabus writers should be careful not to overburden candidates and should bear in mind resources available.

4.4 All syllabuses must describe their content in accordance with the spirit of the examples in Table 1, which show how the above criteria could work in practice in different syllabuses. All syllabuses must make clear that the description of content is not rigidly prescriptive.

▲ *Fig. 5*

ASSESSMENT

Section 5 goes on to look at the techniques of assessment (Fig 6). It starts with an equivocal statement about the issue of differentiation – that is, the way in which assessment can distinguish between the mastery or achievement of the most and least able candidates. In Scotland, where a criterion-referenced examination system at 16+ is also being established, the authorities have, at the time of writing, opted for differentiation through different papers: the pupil must enter for history at one of three levels – foundation, standard or credit. South of the border the feeling is that, if differentiation in history is achieved by this method, we will be little better off than we were in the old days of GCE and CSE; the same invidious distinctions and decisions will be made. So on the one hand there are those who emphasise the need for differentiation through stepped questions or stepped papers where there is an incline of difficulty; on the other hand there are others who are convinced that the only fair way to operate is to have common questions accessible to all abilities where differentiation is done on the basis of the pupils' responses. This difficult issue is dealt with in Chapter 3 on assessment.

The rest of section 5 is concerned with emphasising the range of techniques needed to measure the pupil's achievement across such a diverse collection of assessment objectives. The day has long since passed when the candidates' responses to four or five essay questions selected from a list of say, twenty was considered an adequate way of examining history. In particular, the section emphasises that school-based candidates should now be required to undertake coursework as part of the formal assessment. Such work should carry a minimum of 20 per cent of the total marks. It must be carefully structured and moderated.

The final section of the criteria need not delay us long. The section will eventually be replaced by the grade criteria; at the moment it provides a general indication of the levels of achievement in the assessment objectives likely to be shown by candidates attaining grade F (equivalent to the old CSE grade 4) and grade C (equivalent to the old GCE grade C and the CSE grade 1).

---

5. Techniques of Assessment

5.1 Differentiation will be achieved by the use of differentiated questions within common papers or a combination of differentiated and non-differentiated components within a common set of papers and by setting course work tasks appropriate to candidates' individual levels of ability.

5.2 The range of assessment techniques available in this subject has been considered from the point of view of their fitness for purpose, ie whether or not they are appropriate for the above-stated assessment objectives and taking into account the various needs of candidates throughout the ability range. It is therefore recommended that the following techniques should be included in any scheme of assessment:

(a) questions requiring responses in a variety of forms to given historical evidence;

(b) objective and/or short answer questions which can be used to test both historical knowledge and understanding;

(c) questions demanding an answer written in continuous prose; these questions should take a variety of forms, for example questions based on stimulus materials, parts of structured questions, guided essays, open-ended essays.

Other techniques of assessment are currently used in examining History (eg site descriptions), and should be available to examining groups but the techniques mentioned in (a), (b) and (c) above are, on the basis of available evidence, most effective in testing the stated assessment objectives and, therefore, should attract between them at least 60% of the marks.

Care must be taken to ensure that undue reliance is not placed on any one technique.

5.3 There are some skills and abilities in History which may be assessed as well or better by the use of appropriate forms of course work. Therefore a course work component, carrying a minimum of 20% of the total marks, should normally be required of school-based candidates taking a course in the subject. Clear statements of general course work requirements, which must include the arrangements for proper external moderation, must be provided by the Examining Groups.

▲ *Fig. 6*

THE GENERAL CRITERIA AND THE NATIONAL CRITERIA

The *General Criteria* provide the overall framework which must be taken into account when syllabuses and examinations are drawn up. There are details of the criteria for acceptance of a subject for examination, for the external moderation of school-based work, and the general criteria for all systems of assessment and moderation. The appendices in the *General Criteria* give addresses of the examining groups and a statement of principles for dealing with handicapped candidates. There is also a useful glossary of terms for a single system of examining at 16+. There are, however, three particular areas of importance to history teachers. First, paragraphs 19 (h) and (i) stress that every possible effort must be made to ensure that syllabuses and examinations are free from bias (for example, gender, political or ethnic) and that the multicultural nature of our society must be borne in mind. Second, they make provision for the submission of Mode 2 and 3 examinations, with the criteria for this being laid down. Third, and perhaps most important, the *General Criteria* make it clear that the national criteria (and grade criteria when adopted) are not to ossify. They are to be kept under review by the Secondary Examinations Council and examining groups – a welcome reminder that no one considers that the last word has been said on the history national criteria.

For the moment, however, the published *General Criteria* and *National Criteria – History* provide the blueprint for action, the operational framework which should underwrite the teaching and assessment of history for the 14–16 age range. It will, however, remain a paper exercise, a set of exhortations, unless two groups of people can turn the history criteria into practicalities: those who are concerned with teaching in the classroom and those who must draw up valid and reliable examinations to measure the Assessment Objectives (the examining groups and to a lesser extent the teachers). It is to the teaching that we turn first.

2 Teaching GCSE History

Historians try to describe what the past was like and why things have changed. History teachers and examiners have asked questions about content and concepts of historical time since history examinations began. In this sense, Assessment Objectives 3.1 and 3.2 (see Figure 3 in Chapter 1) seem to be nothing new. The difference is that in the past the ability to recall, evaluate, select and deploy historical information was often tested for its own sake. In GCSE, knowledge will, to a much greater extent, have to be used to fulfil a purpose, such as to put evidence in context, to form the basis of empathetic understanding, or to illustrate historical concepts.

UNDERSTANDING CONCEPTS

It is not yet clear exactly how the new examinations will test the objective of understanding concepts. Certainly we can expect to see a range of types of writing task set, with much less reliance on the long, open essay. Now that this assessment objective has been made explicit, teachers will need to develop the necessary thinking, and the knowledge of terminology, from an early stage.

Similarity and Difference

A consideration of the concepts of similarity and difference can be a good starting-point for the study of a period. A class beginning a study of British social and economic history was given two pictures (Figs 1(a) and (b)), together with the questions which follow (Example A). As with most of the exercises in this chapter, these are best done in groups, with a follow-up class discussion.

Example A

1

	1849	1986
Cooking Lighting Telling the time Heating House decoration		

Copy this table. Complete it for each of the items on the left, for both dates.
2 Add as many other *differences* as you can between the two rooms.
3 Write down any ways in which the two rooms, and their contents, are *the same.*
4 Look more closely at the two pictures. What *materials* are used for cooking and eating utensils, furniture, floor covering etc?
5 In each room, what kind of *energy* would be used for preparing, cooking and eating an evening meal?

▲ *Fig. 1(a) House interior in Wiltshire, 1849*

▲ *Fig. 1(b) Modern kitchen*

The initial listing of differences and similarities will lead into discussions of aspects of continuity and change. Questions 4 and 5 are designed to lead into some of the topics that will form the basis of the course: industrialisation, changes in manufacturing, low and high energy use, etc.

Cause and Consequence

Discussion of the concepts of cause and consequence will probably come at the end of a period of study, rather than the beginning. Experience seems to show that even the basic difference between cause and consequence is not easy to handle. Pupils studying for GCSE exams may be asked to go further into these concepts, and distinguish between short-term and long-term causes, important and less important causes (or results) and so on. Knowledge of the terminology goes a long way towards an understanding of the concept, but students need to learn how to do this in easy situations, in discussion, before facing the commitment of putting things down on paper.

Too often the problems of cause and consequence have become mixed up with problems of factual recall in essay questions such as 'What were the causes of...?' The format below concentrates discussion on the concepts.

Example B

(The class have been studying the Palestinian situation from its origins up to the present day.)

Zionism
Rivalry between Arab states
Palestinians become refugees
Balfour Declaration
Wars of 1956, 1968, 1973
British Mandate
Israelis take over Palestinian farms
Murder of 6 million Jews by Nazis
Terrorism
U.S. support for Jews
Loss of civil rights for Palestinians
Jewish guerrilla groups, e.g. Stern Gang

A Work in groups of four or five.
1 Choose three of the items from the above list which were *causes* of the setting up of the state of Israel in 1948.
2 Choose two of the items from the above list which were *results* of the Israeli victory in 1948 (you may want to include items which you used in question 1).

or B Work in groups of four or five.
1 Choose *one* of the list of items which was, in your opinion, the *most important cause* of the setting-up of the state of Israel in 1948.

2 Choose two of the items on the list which were *long-term causes* of this event.
3 Choose *two* of the items on the list which were *short-term causes* of this event.
4 Choose *one* item which was in your opinion, the *most important result* of the Israeli victory in 1948.

In all cases, explain the reasons for your choice to your group. Reach a group decision, with a spokesperson to explain it to the class.

(Note that some items could appear under more than one list (e.g. terrorism). This doesn't matter, and it is important for the class to know that you do not have any pre-determined 'right answers'. The list above could be split if necessary.)

The ideas involved in such questions are not by any means simple. It seems that many pupils of GCSE age have rather mechanistic models of causation in history. Thus, events follow from each other, and therefore cause each other; such causes mean that key events are 'inevitable'. The problem is developing structures through which the shortcomings of such thinking can be explored. Possible starting questions are:

1 Two reasons for the Communists' victory in China in 1949 were their skill in guerrilla warfare, and their support among the peasants. Both these elements had been present since the late 1930s, so why didn't the Communists win until 1949?
2 After the Long March, was it *inevitable* that the Communists would win in China?

Substantive Concepts

Several GCSE syllabuses indicate that they intend to assess certain substantive concepts, or 'key issues' of history, such as democracy, revolution, monarchy, colonialism or totalitarianism. Clearly there are two approaches to teaching these: either the idea is introduced at the start, and then exemplified, or the examples are discussed and the concept deduced later. Most teachers seem to prefer the second approach and this is how one teacher set about building up the concept of totalitarianism.

Example C

The class studied the outlines of Fascist Italy, Nazi Germany and Stalinist Russia. Pupils in five groups then specialised in finding out about a single aspect of life in all three situations. The groups were: press and broadcasting, young people, opponents, police, industry. Towards the end of the group work the teacher announced that the report back would have to focus on the question: 'How did the state take control of people's lives through the topic you have studied in all three countries?'

Directly after the report-back, brief reference was made, as a contrast, to life in Britain today. The class then worked on similarities and differences between all four situations. At this point the teacher introduced the word 'totalitarianism' and explained what it could mean. This was then used as a reference-point for the pupils' own work. Reinforcement of their understanding was provided through further examples of each of the five topics, drawn from other countries. The first examples were extreme cases (see below). Later examples were less easy to categorise, and led to further discussion of the concept.

- In Country A most of the rulers are army officers and opponents are either in prison or exile.
- In Country B there are several newspapers and TV channels of which only one or two are controlled by the government...
- In Country E there is a youth movement which involves wearing a uniform and swearing an oath of loyalty to the country. Membership is not compulsory, but may be helpful in getting on. The youth movement has a small amount of government money, but is mainly funded by voluntary contributions.

EMPATHY

It is not the function of this book to enter into a discussion of the nature and meaning of empathy. A most useful recent publication does this very well: *Empathy in History – From Definition to Assessment*, published by SREB. Nor is there much point in discussing whether or not it can be done: the national criteria are perfectly plain (see p.12), and all history examinations at GCSE are required to test it. Most schemes do this through coursework although, as methods of assessment improve, it may be that candidates in written examinations will also be asked to show this understanding of how people in the past looked at events and issues.

It might be possible to learn about attitudes and values in the past in the same way as pupils learn about events and situations. However, there must be limitations on this approach: we, and our pupils, are twentieth-century beings, locked into twentieth-century patterns of thought. A full understanding of individual attitudes and values and, through this, a better understanding of motivation can only come through trying to project ourselves into a certain historical situation. It goes without saying that this requires a good, but not necessarily exhaustive, factual knowledge of the place and time in question. The best way to start developing a sense of the perspective of the past is to approach this factual knowledge through primary source material. This encourages projection into the historical situation, enriching it with authentic and concrete details. With most secondary-age pupils the inclusion of visual material, in drawings, paintings or photographs, is important. Music, too, can be a powerful stimulus to reaching an empathetic understanding of the 'otherness' of the past.

Developing Empathy

History teachers have for a long time sought ways to elicit good empathetic responses from their pupils. Often, this has been in the form of the instruction 'Imagine you are...'. Sensitively handled, with adequate preparation, this kind of exercise may still work. However, many of us have been disappointed by the results, probably for two reasons. First, there is no real guidance in such an instruction as to whether to write a work of complete imaginative fiction or simply to recall the facts of the story. Nor is a completely factual piece with an imaginative gloss quite what we are looking for.

Secondly, such an approach may not promote any real historical understanding. Often the task is set for a situation with plenty of emotional appeal: 'Imagine you are an early nineteenth-century worker in textile mill/in a workhouse/in the trenches.' The result may be a colourful piece of writing, and an awareness that situations in which people in the past found themselves could provoke emotional responses. But the attitudes will usually be those of the twentieth century; i.e. how an adolescent of the 1980s would feel if he or she were picked up and dropped into a textile mill, or whatever. Of course there are times when people in the past felt about their situation in exactly the same way as we would, and our common experience of what it means to a human makes this an exciting moment.

However, people in the past also reacted quite differently to their situation. A better piece of historical empathy would answer the question: 'If it was so awful in the textile mill/ workhouse/trenches, why did people choose to work there/live there/join up and stay there?' This could lead to a much fuller historical perspective; in terms of the model given below, it could move the response from the twentieth-century 'everyday' empathy to 'historical' empathy. Filling out the picture by looking at why some First World War soldiers mutinied, why some did not, and why conscription was introduced might move the understanding even deeper into 'differentiated historical empathy' (see below).

The pamphlet produced by the SREB referred to above uses a model of the process which includes four stages:

1 Information gathering
2 Everyday empathy (twentieth-century motives, feelings, and attitudes applied to the past)
3 Stereotyped historical empathy (there is one point of view characteristic of a particular time)
4 Differentiated historical empathy (different groups and individuals in the past had different points of view)

These can be illustrated as shown in Figure 2.

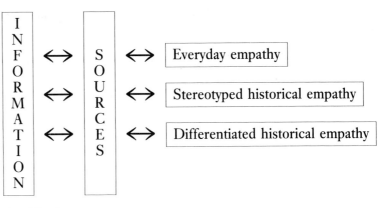

▲ *Fig. 2*

The national criteria for GCSE have implications, of course, for all stages of teaching and learning. Teachers will now be expecting pupils much younger than 14 to begin to understand what empathy is, to distinguish between different types and to write their own empathetic responses. Pupils will need to become familiar with the phraseology used, too. The following exercise has been used with 13-year-olds, and although the question set is very conventional, the point is not in the written accounts produced, but in the discussion of them.

Example D

Eighteenth-century road transport is introduced using some pictures and several primary sources, some very factual – prices, times, distances – some more personal.

1 Write an account of a journey you have made by stage-coach from ____ to London in 1786.
2 In groups, read each others' accounts.
  a) Underline with a wavy line any factual errors in the account.
  b) Underline with a straight line any attitudes or feelings in the account.
  c) Double underline any attitudes or feelings which are based on factual information you know to be correct.
  d) Put a cross in the margin next to any attitudes which you think show 'everyday' empathy – how we would feel today – which you think is not how they felt then.
  e) Put a tick in the margin next to any attitudes which you think they had in the eighteenth century which we do not have now ('historical empathy').

Example E

In another example, this attention to discussion and group work was used to move carefully towards the final piece of written work, this time with 12-year-olds. They were working on Victorian Britain, particularly education and rural life. The teacher was using a considerable amount of local historical material including a school log-book. She focused on a case of truancy: why had the girl played truant? In an initial question-

and-answer session the class offered various ideas; anachronistic and unlikely events were weeded out here. The class broke into groups to discuss it and returned for further discussion as a class. Pupils then wrote short sentences, phrases and jottings for their empathetic work and tried them out on other members of the group. Only after some time did pupils begin to put together their own pieces of extended empathetic writing.

This kind of time-consuming care and tentative, low-risk approach is one that history teachers have not commonly used, but it acknowledges that the development of this skill is not easily achieved.

Drama and role-play

Some of the opportunities and problems of work for this objective can be revealed through drama and role-play. Such work needs careful planning. First, focus the role-play around a genuine historical problem-situation – in the example below, monks and nuns in specific religious houses preparing for the visit of Thomas Cromwell's Commissioners. Then the problem needs to be split up into short specific tasks, to which the groups have to find an answer. At first those answers can be found in the support material for the role-plays, but later in the exercise pupils are forced to consider their own response, in character. In the subsequent discussion, these moments were analysed for examples of 'everyday' or 'historical' empathy.

LESSON PLANS: Sessions 1, 2, and 3 (Team effort, teachers' initials in brackets)

Session 1 (9.25 – 10.35)

1. Introduction. Detectives and evidence. Sherlock Holmes story. (MB) (10 mins)
2. Historians like a detective. Types of sources that the historian uses. List on board. Show examples of these. (SP) (10 mins)
3. Life in monasteries. What information do we have for life in monasteries and nunneries? Pupils make list in books. Report back. List on board. (MB) (10 mins)
4. Examination of some of the information (see. p.25) for monastic life. Photographs, pictures from contemporary books. (SP) (10 mins)
5. Written sources (extract from William of Malmesbury on the Cistercians; extract from a disenchanted monk's letter to Thomas Cromwell, 1535). Read through extracts. Discuss difficult words etc. Remainder of lesson answering questions on worksheet. (MB) (20 mins)

Session 2 (10.55–1200

1. Introduction. Drama session in three East Anglian monasteries and three nunneries. Task to enact the difficulties monastic foundations faced during the reign of Henry VIII. (SP) (5 mins)

2. Distribution of role-cards (monasteries and nunneries will already be set up). Emphasise need to keep true to character and to fill in gaps where information is not provided (e.g. age – occupation of parents – hobbies etc).
   (ALL STAFF) (10 mins)

3. Shopping for a monastery. Laity look round for a suitable house. Heads of houses will interview four laymen and women at a time (chairs to be placed). At the end of interview head will inform candidates whether or not they are accepted. If accepted, go behind head of house; if not look for another house. (SP to introduce – rest of staff to help as necessary) (10 mins)

4. Role casting in the monastery. Novices assume new names and are given tasks within the monastery. (SP direct) (5 mins)

5. Setting the scene for 1535. Stress King's 'divorce'. Acts of Supremacy and Succession. Fears that Chief Minister Cromwell is casting greedy eyes on the monasteries and nunneries because of their wealth. A Visitation is planned. What is the reaction of each house going to be? (5 mins)

6. In role, deciding on reaction to the situation:
   (a) What is monastery or nunnery's reaction to the divorce and break with Rome?
   (b) What will the response be to the Visitation (bribery? lies? honesty? hide wealth? hide the most disreputable monks and nuns? etc, etc) (SP to introduce and direct) (5 mins)

7. The Visitations. MB to be Dr Thomas Legh of Eton and King's, Cambridge; RD or KM to be John Ap Rice.

   KM formally calls each house to the stage to answer the questions the King's Visitors will put to the head of house and monks and nuns. Legh and Ap Rice enter hall to a fanfare of trumpets. Take imposing seats on stage. Each house then comes up in turn to be cross-examined.
   (5 mins per house)

8. If time, announce which houses are to be dissolved. If not, say that announcement will be made next week.

Session 3 (9.25 – 10.35) Next day

1. *Return of homework.* (MB)

2. *Recap on drama session – discussion.* (MB)
   How much can you remember?
   Who were you?
   Which monastery did you join?
   What task did you take on?
   What did it involve?
   What did you feel like when the Commissioners came?

3. *Visitation and the evidence* (SP)
   Map. Report from Thomas Legh and John AP Rice to Thomas Cromwell.

4. *Worksheet* (MB)
   Emphasis on the fact that the historian has to interpret and understand incomplete evidence. Can pupils comment on:

(a) Personalities and behaviour of the Commissioners? The similarities and differences between their position and the monks/nuns?
(b) What were their motives?
(c) Was their judgement just?
(d) What were the motives of Church and State in this action?

Empathy and GCSE Syllabuses

The exercises which follow are designed to set the understanding of empathy in the context of GCSE syllabuses. Pupils will have met the language and concepts of empathy and the model on page 26 before, but need to refine their ideas and apply them to new situations. The exercises as set are designed to develop understanding of empathy through discussion. With some alteration they could become worksheets for small-scale coursework exercises.

Example F

Source 1A ▼ *Fig. 3 Cartoon from* Punch, *1858*

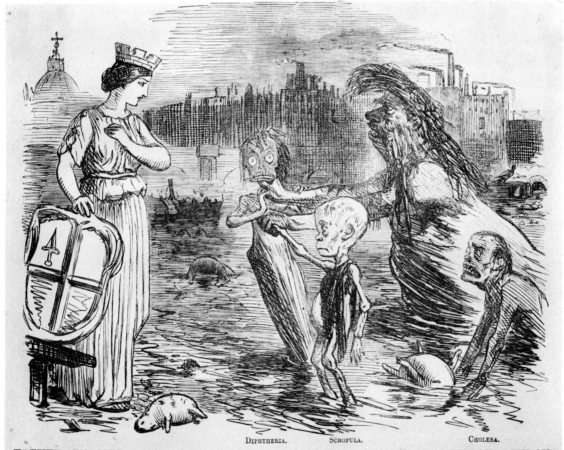

DIPHTHERIA.   SCROFULA.   CHOLERA.

FATHER THAMES INTRODUCING HIS OFFSPRING TO THE FAIR CITY OF LONDON.

Source 1B Report to the Members of the Leeds Board of Health, 1833: 'On 26th May the first case of pure Cholera occurred in the Blue Bell Fold, a small dirty cul-de-sac containing about twenty houses inhabited by poor families. Blue Bell Fold lies on the north side of the river between it and an offensive streamlet which conveys the refuse water from numerous mills and dye-houses.

The first case occurred in a child two years of age which having been in perfect health on the preceding day became suddenly ill on the morning of the 26th and died at 5pm on the same day.

If the Board will refer to the map which accompanies this Report they will at once see how the disease was worst in those parts of the town where there is an entire want of sewage, drainage and paving.' Dr Baker, District Surgeon.

Source 1C ▼ *Fig. 4.*

A COURT FOR KING CHOLERA.

Source 1D From *The Times*, 1853
'We prefer to take our chance with the Cholera than be bullied

into health. There is nothing a man hates so much as being cleansed against his will or having his floors swept, his hall whitewashed, his dungheaps cleared away and his thatch forced to give way to slate. It is a fact that many people have died from a good washing.'

1 What is the attitude of the cartoonist (Source 1A) to public health problems in London?

(This question merely points the student in the direction of seeking evidence of attitudes from the sources. It may be necessary to ask some other questions of this preliminary kind.)

2 The ideas expressed in Source 1D are nonsense to us; why did even an influential paper like *The Times* put forward such views at this time?

(This question tries to point out the contrast between attitudes we hold now and those common in the period in question.)

3 What would be the attitude of the writer of *The Times* article, Source 1D, to the *Punch* cartoon, Source 1A?

4 What do you think would be the attitude of Dr Baker, Source 1B, to the *Punch* cartoon, Source 1A?

(These two questions attempt to explore different attitudes held by different people at the same period – differentiated empathy. In discussion various aspects of this could be developed – why did *The Times* writer feel that way? How could *The Times* still write the way it did twenty years after Dr Baker's report? Etc.)

5 Dr Baker seems to know that disease breeds in dirty conditions, yet the people in Source 1C seem to have little knowledge of hygiene. How do you explain this?

(This question again seeks to look at different attitudes and how they are formed and changed.)

6 Eventually the ideas put forward by people like Dr Baker became widely accepted, and those of *The Times* writer discredited. Why was this so?

(This looks at questions of motive and how attitudes change over time.)

This sequence of questions – which could be considerably extended – is interesting for the range of empathetic ideas which can be explored from quite a small information base. It is the big, wide-ranging 'imaginative writing' question which requires a wide background knowledge in order to be done effectively

It might be thought that the more recent the history that is studied, the more difficult it must be to distinguish between 'everyday' and 'historical' empathy. However there were times, even recently, when attitudes were very different from those held widely today. Indeed it is sometimes only through trying to enter into some sort of empathetic understanding that the historical situation can really be explained. Sometimes this can best be put as a paradox.

Example G   Introduce some factual details of the Munich Agreement and events leading up to the outbreak of the Second World War.

The Munich Crisis of 1938 has been regarded for many years as one of the more shameful episodes of recent British history.

Source 2A ▼ *Fig. 5. Chamberlain at the airport on his return from Munich*

Source 2B From T.A. Neal, Two World Wars, 1972
'In September 1938, the British Prime Minister, Neville Chamberlain, and the French Prime Minister Daladier, agreed at Munich to the German occupation of Sudetenland. Chamberlain's reward was a scrap of paper which he pathetically waved on his return to London. Hitler had personally assured him of his determination not to fight Britain. On the flimsy strength of this Chamberlain proclaimed, "Peace in our time".'

Source 2C Fig. 6.

1 Historians seem to judge the Munich Agreement very critically (Source 2B). How do you explain the attitude of the *Daily Telegraph* (Source 2C)?
2 How far does the attitude of the *Daily Telegraph* explain Chamberlain's own feelings on his return to London?
3 Winston Churchill called the Munich Agreement 'a total and unmitigated defeat'. Explain why Churchill felt this way.

MR. CHAMBERLAIN'S PURPOSE

Braving Europe's Antagonisms to Rescue a Generation from War Fears

ALREADY Mr. Chamberlain has returned from the Munich Conference, bringing his sheaves with him. The harvest that he has reaped is the harvest that he has sown—a harvest of peace.

His coming home has been as swift and sudden as his setting out; and in that little interval of time, measured by the quickened heart-beats of the world, the whole outlook on the future has been transformed.

In his broadcast speech on Tuesday Mr. Chamberlain professed himself a man of peace to the depth of his soul. "Armed conflict between the nations," he said, " is a nightmare to me. . . . I am going to work for peace to the last moment." He has been as good as his word; and to-day he has his reward. Out of the nettle, danger, he has plucked the flower, safety.

▲ *Fig. 6* Daily Telegraph, *1 October 1938*

4 Quite soon after 1938 many people came to agree with Churchill's opinion, rather than the *Daily Telegraph*'s opinion, of the Munich Agreement. How did this come about?

It is the unexpected question which necessitates the further understanding of historical reality: not 'Why do people regard Munich as a sell-out?' but 'Why was the agreement so popular at the time?'

Example H

A similar apparent paradox is provided by some of the propaganda material of the First World War. In this case, understanding of the nature of propaganda contributes to our empathetic understanding of attitudes at the time, and vice versa.

Pupils have studied the nature of the war on the Western Front.

Source 3A Fig. 7.

1 Source 3A suggests that women in Britain in the First World War persuaded their sons, brothers, husbands or other male friends and relations to join the Army, with a strong likelihood of their being killed. How do you explain this?

[A mark scheme for this question would give only low marks to those who took this source at face value, with higher marks for those who raised questions about its reliability as evidence of women's attitudes.]

▲ *Fig. 7 Recruiting poster*

Source 3B Pledge signed by members of the Women of England's Active Service League.
'At this hour of England's peril, I do hereby pledge myself most solemnly in the name of my King and Country to persuade every man I know to offer his service to his country. I also pledge myself never to be seen in public with any man who, being in every way fit and free for service, has refused to respond to his country's call.'

2 Does Source 3B prove that Women in Britain did want men to join up?
3 Why was the poster, Source 3A, designed?

4 What does it tell us about the attitudes of (a) women, (b) those who designed recruiting campaigns, (c) men, in the First World War?

Young people are unlikely to be able to show great insight into historical attitudes and values: they will have only a limited knowledge of human nature. The imperfect nature of empathetic writing has sometimes led teachers to feel that it is not worth doing because it would not be done superlatively well. We perhaps forget that we may set the same pupils a question on the causes of the Second World War without expecting to be able to submit the results for a PhD thesis. Young people have a good deal of experience of empathetic projection in drama, fiction and personal life. The final example illustrates just how important it is to equip them with the capacity to develop disciplined and well-informed empathy.

Example I

Source 4A   (From a Republican newspaper)

Letter from H Block

They show you the excreta on the walls
And tell you how we have done it all
But they don't tell you why
Of taunting screws that made the soft ones cry
They taught us how to cope with dirt
They who have done it long before
When they kicked our slops around the cell floor
And bade us clean it or be beaten more
Call me sir you rebel swine
And on the floor you must dine

A dinner topped with a dirty spit
And tea that smelt of urine
Far better it be to inflict our own thorn
Than to lie down and take it issued with scorn
They can perform cosmetic operations
for visiting British MPs
Who in turn make a cosmetic statement
To put the enquiring population at ease
The propaganda that they spread
is dirtier than our cell wall
But amidst the torture and the dirt
The prisoner he walks tall

Source 4B   (From a Republican newspaper)

Solidarity Greetings

CAMPBELL, Sean: CAMPBELL, Billy. (H-Block). Congratulations, lads, on completing four years on protest. They can't imprison a belief. God bless you all. From Rose and Terry O'Neill and family.

CLARKE, Seamus. (H4-Block). Congratulations to Seamus and Maggie on their engagement. Wishing you both every happiness for the future. From Maria. UTP.

CLARKE, Seamus. (H4-Block). Congratulations to 'Cleaky' and Maggie. You both deserve each other. All the best. Love Andrea. xxx. UTP.

CLARKE, Seamus. (H4-Block). Congratulations to Seamy and Maggie. Wishing you every happiness we would wish for ourselves. From your brother Gerard (H3) and fiancee Kate.

CLARKE, SEAMUS. (H4-Block). Congratulations, Seamus and Maggie, on your engagement. Good luck in your future together. From Seamus Kearney and Seamus Finucane (H3).

CLARKE, Seamus. (H4-block). Congratulations to 'Cleaky' and to Maggie on their engagement. Wishing you both all the happiness you truly deserve. God bless. From Micky (H3) and Treasa.

CLARKE, Seamus. (H4-Block). Congratulations to Maggie and 'Cleaky' on their engagement. Wishing you every happiness. From the 'jet-setter' Finook.

McCOMB, Eugene. (H5-Block). Congratulations, son, on completing four years on the blanket. "Never shall we see their like again, not in a thousand years, for their courage is our guiding light, the blanket volunteers." Thinking of you always, from your mammy, dad, and sister Elizabeth. Victory to our hunger-strikers.

McCOMB, Eugene. (H5-Block). Congratulations, Eugene, on completing four years on the blanket for political status. "It is not those who can inflict the most, but those who can endure the most, who will ultimately be the victors." From Betty, Paddy, and family. Victory to the blanket men.

McCOMB, Eugene. (H5-Block). Congratulations, brother on completing four years on the blanket. I knew you could do it. Victory to the blanket men. Victory to the hunger-strikers. From Damien and Teresa.

1 Could you do what these prisoners have done?
2 How do you explain their motives?
3 What factors helped them to carry on so long?

EVIDENCE

Weighing up the evidence, Source-Book, Evidence in History, History from Sources, History Evidence Series, Sources Pack – these are just some of the titles publishers have produced in the last few years. Clearly they have felt that, somehow, history teachers wanted more from their textbooks than a narrative. The onset of GCSE and the detailed Assessment Objective 3.4 (Chapter 1, Fig. 4) in the *National Criteria* have added to the flood of titles.

Nearly all history teachers would now agree that, in history, 'statements are made which are provisional, yet which are derived from evidence' (*National Criteria – History*, para. 1.2). For a long time teachers have used pictures, eyewitness accounts or artefacts to illustrate an event, enliven a topic and add that special sense of reality that distinguishes history from fiction. Examiners have used documentary sources as a stimulus to test candidates' knowledge of history. But the *National Criteria* are now demanding something more than illustration or stimulus: they demand that pupils acquire the skills necessary to use evidence.

Whether a source contains evidence, and the nature of that evidence, only becomes clear when it is questioned. For example, Figure 8 can provide evidence for several kinds of investigation:

▲ *Fig. 8 Working in the fields in Suffolk, 1870s*

- farm implements in use
- farming methods
- clothes worn by farm workers
- jobs done by men
- styles of photography
- techniques of photography
- landscape history

It is also, for us, evidence of the range of questions which can be usefully asked about one historical source.

The Nature of Evidence

It is the question put by the historian which decides whether or not a source contains useful evidence. It also determines the nature of that evidence – whether it is primary or secondary, reliable or unreliable, biased or unbiased, and so on. The distinction between primary and secondary sources, for example, is often spoken of as if it were an absolute distinction. Consider the following three items:

A A contemporary newspaper article about an election in Greece, based on a press agency report.
B The drawing, Figure 10 (on p. 42)

C The textbook *World Powers in the 20th Century,* by Harriet Ward, published in 1978.

Are these primary or secondary sources? Answer: The kind of evidence they will yield depends on the question asked. Item A is secondary evidence of events in Greece, but a primary source of evidence for British interest in foreign news. Item B is a secondary source of evidence about events in Russia in 1917, but it is a primary source for attitudes in Russia in the 1930s. Item C is an obvious secondary source, but it is also a primary source of teachers' views of what should be taught in the 1970s about contemporary history.

Consider the extract from G.F. Alexandrov, *J.V. Stalin,* Moscow, 1947:

> J.V. Stalin is the genius, the leader and teacher of the Party, helmsman of the Soviet state and captain of the armies... Everybody is familiar with his modesty, his simplicity of manner, his consideration for the people, and his merciless severity towards the enemies of the people.
>
> Stalin is the worthy continuer of the cause of Lenin, or, as it is said in the Party: Stalin is the Lenin of today.

Is this reliable or unreliable? Answer: It depends on the question being asked. It is unreliable evidence about Stalin's personality, but it is reliable evidence of the nature of Stalinist propaganda.

Teaching Methodological Skills

It is not possible here to go into all the methodological skills which are involved in studying evidence. Certainly the range of concepts and of types of source which pupils might be asked to handle can be quite demanding. Clearly schools will need to adopt a developmental approach from the time pupils start to learn history and not leave the whole structure until the beginning of the GCSE course. A useful strategy is to break down the skills into clear, single ideas, and design materials to teach these.

Some teachers have found it helpful to examine common fallacies which pupils tend to hold at the early stages, and use simple, clearly-designed tasks to provide a basis for talking them through these. The more common fallacies seem to be:

> Eyewitness accounts must be reliable.
> Contemporary accounts must be eyewitness accounts.
> Secondary evidence is less reliable than primary.
> Secondary evidence is less useful than primary.
> Reliable evidence must be useful.
> Biased evidence must be useless.
> Reliable evidence must be unbiased.
> Biased evidence must be unreliable.

Several of these points will be dealt with in the exercises which follow, but the most useful thing for a book on GCSE to do is to take the Assessment Objectives from the *National Criteria* and see how these could be developed. We shall start by taking the skills outlined in 3.4.1, 3.4.2 and 3.4.3 (see Chapter 1, Figure 4) and then look over how different types of sources pose their own problems.

Objective 3.4.1 refers to 'comprehending and extracting information'. This is something that examiners have often done, but must lead us to consider the difference between sources as information and sources as evidence.

Example J

1 Which unions are referred to in the cartoon (Figure 9)

▲ *Fig. 9 Cartoon from* Punch

2 What does this cartoon tell us about attitudes in Britain in 1921 towards the 'Triple Alliance' of unions?
(Question 1 uses the source as information; Question 2 uses it as evidence. One could go on to follow the line of Question 2 a little further.)

3 Is this source a primary or a secondary source of evidence about industrial attitudes in 1921?
4 Do you think this source represents the unions' or the employers' view of the 'Triple Alliance'? How is this bias shown?
5 What questions would you want to ask in order to decide if this cartoon is a reliable source of evidence about attitudes in Britain in 1921?

The information/evidence distinction can be made in a different way by looking at a source, such as Figure 3 (page 29). This has almost no informational value at all, except perhaps for the coat of arms of the City of London and the dome of St Pauls in the background. It is however, interesting and useful evidence of changing attitudes to public health in Britain at the time.

Objective 3.4.2 introduces interpretation skills, firstly distinguishing between fact, opinion and judgement. The difference between 'opinion' and 'judgement' can sometimes be subjective, but perhaps it is a matter of substantiation: an opinion lacks factual support, a judgement has factual substantiation.

Example K

Source 5A From the *British Gazette*
'How London is Fed.
Raising the Siege at the Docks.
Twenty armoured cars and one hundred food lorries.
A long line of motor lorries swinging into Hyde Park during the weekend bore witness to the fact that the strike had suffered an early defeat in this attempt to starve London.'

Source 5B From the *British Worker*
'I learnt from one of the dockers' pickets that about one hundred and fifty tons of meat had been taken one night from one of the ships and were now being moved by this unnecessary display of force.
  The men, whose normal work is to handle thousands of tons of such cargo each day, lined the streets with arms folded, smiling and chatting, waving a greeting to the soldiers.'

1
Fact	Opinion	Judgement

Draw the table above on to a full page. For both Sources 5A and 5B find as many examples as you can of facts, opinions

and judgements and write them in the correct column. For any judgements that you find, put the facts on which the judgement is based in brackets underneath.
2 Source 5A makes the whole operation sound very serious – a military exercise. How do the opinions and judgements create this impression?
3 Do the facts in Source 5A also contribute to this impression? Explain your answer.
4 What impression of the event is given in Source 5B?
5 How do the opinions and judgements in that Source contribute to that impression?
6 How do the facts in Source 5B also contribute to that impression?
7 The *British Gazette* was the Government newspaper in the General Strike; why did they want to create the impression they did?
8 The *British Worker* was the TUC newspaper in the General Strike; why did they want to create the impression they did?
9 In groups, discuss the part played by facts, opinions and judgements in creating an impression in a newspaper account of an event. Focus on *facts*: how can facts be biased?

The objective then moves on to 'deficiencies in the material as evidence, such as gaps and inconsistencies' – in other words, questions of reliability.

▲ *Fig. 10 Drawing made in 1935 showing Lenin and Stalin together in 1917. Lenin is seated far left, Stalin is sitting next to him. They are talking with a sailor, seated with his back to us, a soldier with a cap in his hand, and a peasant, with a hat on, in the presence of several other men.*

Example L

Source 6 Fig. 10.
The class is studying Stalin and the cult of personality.
1 What impression of the relationship between Lenin and Stalin is given in this drawing?
2 What in fact was the relationship between Lenin and Stalin in 1917?
3 What did Lenin say about Stalin in his *Testament* of 1922?
4 Is this source a reliable source of evidence for events in Russia in 1917? Explain your answer.
5 This source is a piece of propaganda from 1935 : what is it saying about Stalin that would help him?
6 This source is therefore a reliable source of evidence about propaganda in Russia in 1935; how can a source be both reliable and unreliable?

This objective concludes with 'detecting bias.' Examples of biased sources have already been given – Example L, on Source 6, for example, could be extended to investigate questions of bias. However, it might be better to approach bias through graded exercises. After all, the two words 'detecting bias' cover many types of bias – blatant prejudice, bias by use of loaded language, bias by omission or selection of facts, unwitting bias through simply not having all the information available, and so on.

Example M

Source 7A Richard Oastler, letter to the *Leeds Mercury*, 1830
'Thousands of our fellow creatures, both male and female, the inhabitants of a Yorkshire town are at this moment existing in a state of slavery more horrid than are the victims of that hellish system, colonial slavery. The very streets ... are wet by the tears of innocent victims at the accursed shrine of greed who are compelled ... by the dread of the strap of the overlooker to hasten half-dressed, but not half-fed, to those magazines of British Infantile Slavery – the worsted mills in the town and neighbourhood of Bradford.'

Source 7B From the records of a Parliamentary Select Committee
– At what time in the busy time did those girls go to the mills?
– At the busy time they were gone at three o'clock in the morning and ended at 10 at night.
– Had you not great difficulty in awakening your children at this excessive hour?
– Yes, in the early time we had to take them up asleep and shake them, and when we got them on the floor to dress them, before we put them off to work.
– Have your children ever been strapped?
– Yes, every one. My eldest daughter, when my wife came in she said her back was beaten nearly to a jelly.

1. What is the attitude of Richard Oastler (Source 7A) to child labour in the mills?
2. What does he compare the child workers to?
3. Give three other examples of emotive language used by Oastler.
4. The evidence in Source 7B is primary evidence from the records of a Parliamentary Select Committee. Does that mean it is reliable?
5. Does that mean it is unbiased?
6. We know that some members of the Short-Time Committees (a pressure-group working to cut factory hours) rehearsed source witnesses in their evidence. Does that mean that this evidence is unreliable?
7. Evidence such as Source 7B was published by the people who wanted to cut factory hours, as part of their campaign. Can we still say that Source 7B is unbiased evidence?
8. What kind of evidence would you want to see before making up your mind about child labour in factories in the early nineteenth century?
9. Which is the more effective piece of propaganda against child labour, Source 7A or Source 7B? Give reasons for your answer.

The final detailed objective in the *National Criteria* asks pupils to compare 'different types of historical evidence and reach conclusions based on this comparison.' This is perhaps curiously expressed: one does not have to compare different *types* of evidence (rather an abstruse skill anyway) in order to reach conclusions; comparisons of different pieces of evidence of the same type can be equally useful in reaching conclusions. However, this is clearly a distinct area, dealing with the nature of proof, truth and provisional truth in history. We also want to look at the assumption, held by many students, that the truth lies halfway between two conflicting pieces of evidence.

Example N

Let us go back to Sources 5A and 5B (page 40) and add Source 5C – a photograph of the event (Fig. 11).

1. Make two columns, headed 'Source 5A' and 'Source 5B'. Write under each heading any item from the source which is supported by the photograph, Source 5C (Fig. 11).
2. Rule across the page, then write under each heading any item from the source which is contradicted by the photograph.
3. How far does the photograph help you decide which of these two sources is the more accurate?
4. So far we have taken Source 5C as totally correct and accurate. In what ways might photographs give an impression of an event which was either (a) inaccurate or (b) misleading?
5. In groups, discuss what you know of this event in 1926. Write down known facts, and your own judgements. Then write an agreed account of the event. Which of the Sources, 5A, or 5B does your account come closest to?

▲ *Fig. 11 The General Strike, 1926*

The opening paragraph of this objective mentions 'a wide variety of historical evidence.' The skills we have been discussing so far will have to be applied to the different types of sources quoted. This may be very difficult: detecting bias in some statistical sources would be quite beyond the abilities of this writer at least. Teachers may need to develop new skills in this area, as well as in other less frequently used types of sources, such as artefacts and oral evidence.

In many ways all types of sources can be treated in more or less the same way. (Although there are, of course, some variations: one doesn't ask whether an iron-age loom-weight is biased.)

Example O

Source 8 Adapted from G. Kitson Clark, *The Making of Victorian England*, 1965.
'Suitable housing did not exist, and the additional number were crammed into every nook and cranny from attic to cellar of old decaying property, or into little cottages run up hastily in confined spaces with little or no access to light and air. Water and sanitation were often not provided at all, and where they

were provided there was often a mixture of cesspools and wells, with an occasional over-stocked graveyard or active slaughterhouse ... Since many industries now used coal furnaces and most domestic fires burned coal, from many towns a heavy sulphurous smoke cloud was emitted to combine with other atmospheric conditions to make the fogs which were such a feature of Victorian England, and which probably slew thousands.'

1 How can you tell this is a secondary source of evidence for life in cities in Victorian Britain?
2 What kinds of primary sources has the author used to write this source?
3 The author has used a great deal of primary sources about Victorian Britain; does that mean his account is likely to be very reliable? Does this mean that his account is likely to be unbiased?

There are special problems in considering visual material, some of which have already been examined in some of the questions on Sources 5C and 6. Fiction, too, poses interesting problems when considered as historical evidence, or as historical interpretation.

Example P

The following worksheet was based on a video of the Channel 4 programme *Ishi, The Last of His Tribe* and is included here to show some of the kinds of questions which can be asked.

The story is set in the late nineteenth century: it describes a survivor of a mountain Indian tribe, persecuted by white hunters and befriended by a white anthropologist.

1 What skills did Ishi have?
2 In what ways were the customs and beliefs of his tribe different from those of the whites?
3 What were his feelings about the whites? (Give examples.)
4 What attitudes did the whites in the film have towards Indians? (Give examples.)

Read the following sources:
Source 9A George Catlin, *Letters and Notes on the Manners, Customs and Condition of the North American Indians*, Vol. 1, Wiley & Putman, New York, 1841.
'From what I have seen of these people I say there is nothing very strange in their character. It is a simple one, and easy to be understood if the right means be taken to familiarize ourselves with it. The North American Indian in his native state is an honest, faithful, brave, warlike, cruel, revengeful, relentless – yet honourable, contemplative and religious being. From the very many acts of their hospitality and kindness, I pronounce them, by nature, a kind and hospitable people.'
Source 9B Horace Greeley, *An Overland Journey from New York to San Francisco in the Summer of 1859,* Alfred A. Knopf, 1964
'The Indians are children. Their wars, treaties, habitations, crafts, comforts, all belong to the very lowest ages of human existence. Squalid and conceited, proud and worthless, lazy and lousy, they will strut out or drink out their miserable existence, and at length afford the world relief by dying out of it.'

5 What is the attitude of *each* source to the Indians?
6 Do you think the makers of the film would agree with Source 9A or Source 9B? Explain your answer.
7 Does that mean that one of the sources is wrong? Explain your answer.
8 The film was made in 1984, long after the events it shows are supposed to have happened and even longer after Sources 9A and 9B were written. Does this mean that the film must be wrong in what it says of Indian life?
9 How do you think the film-maker made it so convincing?
10 Which of the three – film, Source 9A or Source 9B – do you think is the most *truthful* account of Indian life? Give reasons for your answer.

DIFFERENTIATION IN THE CLASSROOM

The injunction in the *General Criteria*, para. 16, that examinations must be designed 'so that candidates across the ability range are given opportunities to demonstrate their knowledge, abilities and achievements' has had as profound an effect on history examinations as the subject criteria themselves. So far all syllabuses in history for all examining groups have chosen to set common papers and to 'differentiate by outcome' or by incline of difficulty. The teacher in the classroom is obviously also required to encourage positive achievement (surely, we always have tried to do this anyway?). However, a teacher is not under the same constraints as an examiner: all the range of options – differentiated tasks, extension work, inclines of difficulty as well as common tasks – can be used, as appropriate.

In some situations, pupils studying history for GCSE may be grouped by ability. In others, external pressures such as falling rolls, or the opportunity presented by a common examination, may lead to mixed-ability groups. In either situation, teachers may choose to use different strategies at different times.

Most of the teaching material in this chapter was designed for, and has been used with, the full range of abilities in comprehensive schools. Most of the questions, therefore, are ones to which all abilities of pupils might be expected to make some kind of positive response. Teachers may want to modify the language used in some questions, probably, although we should remember that poor readers are not necessarily poor thinkers.

The two sets of questions in Example B on cause and consequence in the Palestinian situation (page 22) could be used with sheet A as a class exercise, and sheet B as extension work for more able pupils. They could also be combined to form a single worksheet which could have an incline of difficulty. The worksheet in Example K on fact, opinion and judement (page 40) may perhaps have an incline of difficulty, although the teacher who designed it feels that all pupils could make some positive response to all questions.

The work of the teacher moves closer to that of the examiner in coursework (see the *National Criteria,* para 5.3, page 18). The requirement to differentiate is all the sharper, of course, but teachers can still use the fullest possible range of types of assignment.

COURSEWORK

The rationale for making coursework a compulsory element in all history courses is that some objectives are more appropriately assessed in coursework. This is certainly true, but the coursework element, at least 20 per cent, but commonly 30 per cent or 40 per cent (and even more in some Mode 2 and Mode 3 courses), is also an opportunity for some different types of teaching and learning to take place. It is an opportunity to take the requirements of the syllabus and tailor them to the specific needs and interests of the class or the teacher. It is an opportunity for students, too, to show what they can do with the stress of the exam removed.

The examining groups appear to have somewhat different ideas about the nature of coursework: is it one or two pieces of work, of some length, meeting several assessment criteria (MEG, SEG) or is it a batch of shorter pieces of work, meeting the range of assessment criteria collectively (LEAG, NEA plus all Schools History Project syllabuses)? Clearly there are merits in both approaches.

The Single (or Double) Large-scale Investigation

Advantages

This type of investigation offers more scope for personal, original work. Teachers may feel that it can fulfil other objectives of their own – for example the development of certain study skills. It could encourage pupils to do something like 'real historical research.'

Disadvantages

It may be difficult to set up personal investigations for every member of a class, or several classes. The open-ended investigation is a risky enterprise if it is genuine original research: the student may come to a dead end and not produce a worthwhile-looking assignment. On such large-scale pieces of work it may be harder to ensure that certain required objectives are met. It may also be difficult to decide how much help to give a student – or indeed how much outside help he or she has received. Pupils may also be under pressure to put time into coursework assignments in several other subjects. Most of all, it may be difficult to fit the time for such an investigation into the 5½ terms of the course: some GCSE syllabuses do not seem to be any smaller than their predecessors, and coverage still seems to be important.

The Small-scale Coursework Assignment

Advantages

It may be possible to design coursework assignments so that they arise out of the syllabus and the normal course of study. They are then, in a real way, *course*work, and no time is lost. Individual assignments can be focused on one or two objectives, so that specific skills are clearly and visibly assessed. It may be possible for candidates to do several pieces of work around a particular objective, and to submit the best for final assessment. It may also be easier to ensure comparability of candidates across short assignments, and the candidate who has had bad luck over a piece of work has not lost too much. It may also be easier to account for outside assistance.

Disadvantages

Students will not have the pleasure and satisfaction of carrying out a lengthy investigation. The administration and working of several assignments will probably be more complicated. It is also harder for very able candidates to score highly across several pieces of work: this pattern may reward consistency as much as brilliance.

Assessment Objectives

Having decided which style of coursework to adopt, teachers will need to look closely at which Assessment Objectives are to be met through coursework. It would also be worth finding out, at the earliest possible stage, what the different examining groups mean by certain objectives. This book, for example, has a certain view of what empathy is: does your group feel the same way? How would they define a good response to the coursework assessment objectives?

It may be that these issues will have been made clear at the Phase IV in-service training sessions. It is probably advisable for teachers to keep in contact with examining groups, and with colleagues doing the same syllabus, over their first few years of GCSE. This is a new examination, assessing things that have not often been assessed before, and we can expect quite an amount of change at the beginning.

It is certainly important to be clear what the Assessment Objectives mean, and how they could be met, at the stage when assignments are being designed. They are not simply to be applied to coursework when it has been written. Once coursework assignments have been designed to meet these objectives, and to develop the best responses, they should be made explicit to students at the time they are set. The point is not to set up an abstruse game in which only the assessor knows all the rules, but to allow students, through coursework, to show what they know, understand and can do.

Some of the examining groups' coursework arrangements make it necessary to assess more than one objective in any individual assignment. However, where possible it is best to stick to one objective per assignment. At first sight this may seem a waste. An assignment such as: 'Read the following sources and describe the impact of the coming of the railways on people in towns in Victorian Britain' may clearly fulfil at least three objectives: analysis of sources; empathy; cause and consequence. However, will it be possible for candidates to perform at a high level in all three of these skills? The group of sources may simply have to be read and understood; the empathetic writing involved in many students' answers may be quite perfunctory, if it is visible at all. Of course, these skills may well have been used by the candidate in answering the assignment question, but the one objective which will probably be most demonstrably fulfilled will be an understanding of the nature of cause and consequence. It will do candidates more justice to give all the marks available to this objective, and save the assessment of empathy or evidence skills for an assignment which can be specifically designed to elicit good responses to them. A single assessment pattern also makes life simpler for the students, for your administrative and marking load, and, eventually, for the assessor.

In order to give sharpness to an assignment, to direct students to the particular skill to be assessed, it is often useful to subdivide the task. Thus, if the actual skill to be assessed requires some analysis of the role of an individual in history, better results might be obtained by asking students to undertake the kind of assignment shown in Example Q.

Example Q

Read the text about Custer [page references given].
1 For *each* of the following 'decision-points' (i–iii), say:
   (i)   9.25 p.m., 24 June 1876
   (ii) 8.00 a.m., 25 June 1876
   (iii) 3.00 p.m., 25 June 1876

   (a) What choices did Custer face?
   (b) What did he do?
   (c) What do you think were his reasons for this decision?

2 From your answers to question 1, what do you think were Custer's motives and personality?
3 How does the rest of his career fit in with this conclusion?
4 In what ways did Custer affect the history of the Plains Indians in the nineteenth century?
5 In what ways would the history of the American West have been different without Custer?

Many of the exercises described in the earlier parts of this chapter could be used as coursework assignments if the syllabus requires a number of shorter pieces of work. Extended assignments could also benefit from being directed at various points.

Example R

Suffragettes and votes for women
Your project on this topic is worth 20 per cent of the marks. You will work on it for five weeks, including homeworks. You will be expected to work on your own, or in groups, but you must see your teacher at least once a week to show how you are getting on.

For this project you have to show that you can:

(i) carry out an investigation on your own
(ii) collect information in answer to a question
(iii) analyse and interpret sources of evidence
(iv) carry out a piece of empathetic writing.

Information available [given].

1 After one lesson, make a list of the questions on this topic which you want to find the answers to. Keep this list, and add other questions as you go along. It will be marked alongside your finished project.
2 You must at some point, do one of the EVIDENCE exercises, 'The Suffragette Derby' or 'The Suffragettes and the Rest of the Country'. These two packs, with questions, are in [given].
3 You must do *one* of the following:
  (a) Write a speech which a suffragette might make in her own defence after being taken to court for smashing windows in the High Street.   *or*
  (b) Following the Suffragette Derby of 1912, write a speech given by an MP explaining why he is against votes for women.   *or*
  (c) Explain the reactions of a suffragist to the militant suffragette campaign.
4 You must answer one of the following questions at the end of your project:
  (a) Did the suffragettes have widespread popular support among women?   *or*
  (b) Do you regard the suffragette movement as a success or a failure?

Example S

Local study
Objectives: Personal investigation of a site
            Relating a site to its context
            Empathy

[The class have looked at slides and pictures of houses in class, and have visited some sites all together, with the teacher. They are then split into groups of two to four, and each group is given a section of the town centre containing about 12–15 buildings.]

1 For each building, make a sketch, with labels, of the main features. Use the recording sheets for other notes of materials, uses etc.
  (a) What clues are there to tell you the period in which it was built?
  (b) Add your own suggestions for the date of the buildings, with your reasons.
2 Choose one of the buildings [a list of ten nineteenth-century

buildings, private and public]. Analyse and record it as in activity 1. List the clues which tell you it is a nineteenth-century building. Is it all entirely nineteenth-century?

[Back at school. A box of information has been prepared, including secondary sources about Britain in the nineteenth century in general, as well as this town in particular, and multiple copies of some primary sources – directories, census returns (including the religious census), newspaper articles.]

3 Using the information provided, try to answer the following questions for the building you have chosen:
  (a) Who built it? For what reasons?
  (b) What does this building tell us about the town of _____ at the time?

4 Choose one of the families from the 1851 census return. Use your imagination and all the information you have learnt about life in the nineteenth century to write a day in the life of one (or more) of the members of the family.

Planning and Administration

It is worth planning the placing and duration of the coursework within the 5½-term course, and, in schemes where the number and weighting of different assignments is at the teacher's discretion, making an outline of these before the course starts. In some cases, centres are required to get in touch with their examining groups fairly early in the course (during fourth-year work, for example). There are advantages in this for the centre: finding out exactly what the examiners have in mind, making early contact with your coursework assessor, even having your assignment titles vetted. Teachers will, of course, need to reserve the right to alter assignments, and weightings, as the course progresses: better ideas will appear, assignments may not work as intended, timings may go astray etc.

Coursework assignments should also have a mark scheme prepared at the same time as the questions. Teachers are required to 'differentiate' in their coursework marking, just as the written examinations are required to do (see Chapter 3). The different examining groups offer advice on this in different ways, and this is another reason for making early and close contact with them. It is probably advisable to mark coursework assignments as they are completed, but to check these marks at the time when the whole coursework package has to be prepared for external moderation or assessment.

There are advantages to a centre in the new, closer, relationship many will be making with the examiners, through coursework, in being as administratively efficient as possible. Assignments are best retained by the teacher, once they have been completed and marked. Where two or more teachers are involved in taking groups for GCSE, there are benefits in holding an internal standardisation meeting (even where this is not required anyway). The deadlines, the arithmetic and the paperwork are worth getting right. There are also advantages both for your candidates, and for your coursework assessor in providing, for each assignment, a small supporting package of documents: the title and worksheets, a note of how much time and how much guidance was given, a note of what supporting material was available, and under what circumstances (at home, in class) the work was done, together with mark schemes.

3 Assessment in GCSE History

IMPORTANCE OF CRITERIA

The messages contained within the GCSE subject-specific criteria for history, and indeed for any subject for which criteria exist, will mean nothing and hence will achieve nothing until two things happen. First, the development of teaching and learning strategies which can meet the criteria in the classroom and, second, the development of assessment which can evaluate and make judgements about student performance in relation to the criteria. Both these will involve those actually teaching the students, as Chapter 2 makes clear, but the second will also involve the five GCSE examining groups.

One of the features which distinguishes the GCSE from the two examinations it replaces (GSE O Level and CSE) is the close interrelationship that exists between the curriculum and the examining process. It is absolutely essential therefore that there is no mismatch between the criteria (themselves subject to ongoing review) and the GCSE examination. There will exist a wide range of different teaching and learning strategies designed to meet the criteria and to provide evidence upon which pupil performance in relation to these criteria can be judged. Such strategies cannot of course be confined to a two-year slice of secondary schooling or to a single subject. The GCSE will in consequence have significant long-term implications for whole-school curriculum and assessment planning, both pre-14 and for the 14–18 age range, whatever the patterns of secondary education may be in particular parts of the country.

DIFFERENTIATION – AIMS AND PRINCIPLES

For both teacher and examiner, the key issue in the GCSE is differentiation. This simply means that all students (and GCSE is intended to be accessible to over 80 per cent of the population) will be able to show what they know, understand and can do. Differentiation is thus concerned with positive achievement.

One of the worst features of current public examinations is their largely negative impact. The reasons for this are complex, but sufficient to say here that they stem in large measure from the widespread use of public examinations in this country for selection purposes. The examination model used is thus largely norm-referenced and hence makes its comparisons between individuals using an uninformative grading scale, which permits simplistic judgements to be made about and between students. The implications of this for assessment design are unfortunate, since it results in the setting of questions and the posing of problems which are designed to ensure that substantial numbers of students will not be able to answer them. When O level or CSE chief examiners say that they have set a good discriminating question, they actually mean that they have set a question which 70 per cent of candidates won't be able to answer and the examiners intend that this is what will happen.

This rationale for question-setting is further reinforced by a marking methodology, which, as far as history is concerned, encourages two things. First, the notion that there is somehow a correct answer to every question, and secondly, the creation of mark schemes based on model answers. Such schemes provide a basis against which the work of any candidate can be judged according to the degree to which it has matched or failed to match the model answer. Quite apart from ensuring that no one can ever gain full marks, such a procedure ensures that the lowest marks are awarded on the basis of how much worse the answers provided are in comparison with the model, and hence with the best answers.

The above description of norm-referenced assessment is to some degree an exaggeration, in order to make a point, but not much. A few current O level and CSE examinations, notably the Schools History Project (SHP), formerly *History 13–16*, have developed different approaches to both marking and question-setting in recent years, which is not surprising in SHP's case, as it has been delivering the national criteria for over a decade.

The challenge facing assessment for GCSE in history is how to shift an assessment model involving both setting and marking which at present discriminates negatively between some 60 per cent of the school population to one which differentiates positively between some 80 per cent. This shift has moreover to be made, as Chapters 1 and 2 have made clear, in relation to criteria which stress skills and concepts at the expense of reproducing information learnt for its own sake. In particular, the history criteria stress the key concepts of cause and consequence, continuity and change, similarity and difference (para. 3.2), the skills necessary to study historical sources and to use them as evidence (para. 3.3), and the development of empathy (para. 3.4) – see Chapter 1, Figures 2 and 3 (page 12). This, again, is quite a significant change as far as public examining in history is concerned, where the direct testing of skills and concepts has not in the past attracted a particularly high weighting.

The history criteria moreover do not specify any particular model for differentiation, nor the use of any specific techniques of assessment. The relevant criteria here are to be found in section 5 (see Chapter 1, Figure 6, page 18), where the only statements which border on the prescriptive are those contained in Note II, which states, 'prescribed documents would not satisfy objective 3.4 and are therefore not recommended', and criterion 5.3, which reads, inter alia, 'therefore a coursework component carrying a minimum of 20 per cent of the total marks should normally be required of school based candidates taking a course in the subject'. It is therefore possible for the examining groups to use any model of differentiation in history, from one which sets common questions, all of which have to be answered by all candidates, to one which uses completely separate papers designed for candidates at different points along the grade scale. The most extreme example of this last approach in actual use in the GCSE is the four-paper model proposed for mathematics. Moreover, the Secondary Examinations Council (SEC), which has overall responsibility for seeing that the GCSE examinations implement the criteria, after initially favouring differentiation through separate papers has subsequently pursued a commendably even-handed approach to differentiation. In coming to this view, SEC incidentally made use of evidence provided by SHP that common questions could differentiate effectively in a subject like history.[1]

The only requirement therefore is that the model used for differentiation should indeed differentiate, and it needs to be stressed that all approaches have their own problems and difficulties. In practice, history has chosen a model well towards the common end of the spectrum, and no GCSE examination in history proposes to use separate papers. Philosophically, common assessment is attractive, since it seems to many people to be the only way to avoid recreating the old GCE O level/CSE divide. All the 16+ feasibility studies in history going back to the mid-1970s had used common assessment and had experimented with varying ways of structuring questions (about which more later). Most history teachers, however, and hence examiners, cannot bring themselves to abandon choice in examinations, although the arguments for doing so are becoming increasingly powerful. There was also considerable concern about the effects upon both ends of the ability range of asking exactly the same question of every student.

The result of these conflicting views has inevitably been a compromise and has led to the extensive use in GCSE history of written papers in which all the questions remain open to all students, but in which an incline of difficulty is built either into parts of the same question, or into successive questions. These so-called stepped questions or stepped papers are not in practice well suited to the delivery of positive assessment, since it is impossible to determine difficulty in any overall sense. Such a model is bound to expose students to questions they cannot answer in positive terms, and which moreover examiners to not intend that they should. The following is an example of a stepped question.

Example 1

(i) What name is usually applied to the system of improving Soviet industry during the years covered by the industrial statistics in Source D? (1)
(ii) Describe the main features in the working of this system. (2)
(iii) How do the industrial statistics (Source D) show some of the priorities in the system and the success it achieved? (4)

[1] *Differentiation by outcome in History*. A feasibility study and report to the SEC, October 1985.

The industrial statistics provided in Source D cover five major areas and refer to the years 1928, 1933 and 1940. The marks reflect the examiner's view of the relative weighting of the part questions, and, since they are printed on a question paper, they cannot be changed – however the question may work in practice. It is worth asking incidentally whether a mark as low as 4 is justified for Part (iii), given the demands of the question. Genuine differentiation can probably only really be achieved through the use of common questions allied to positive marking, or to specific questions targeted at relatively restricted ranges of ability expressed in grade terms. To date the differentiation debate in history has been almost entirely centred around written questions, and little thought has so far been given to the very considerable opportunities for achieving differentiation through coursework.

PATTERNS OF ASSESSMENT

The overall pattern of assessment proposed by the various examining group for GCSE has also been remarkably similar and consists typically of two timed examination papers occupying approximately three hours altogether, and a coursework component carrying a weighting of between 20 and 40 per cent (most often the former). Sometimes one of the two written papers (usually the first and longer of the two) is split into two parts. The second, and shorter, of the two papers is almost always concerned with source-based questions designed to test comprehension, evaluation and interpretation. The only groups, to break significantly with this pattern have been the Welsh Joint Education Committee (WJEC) and the Northern Ireland Schools Examinations Council (NISEC) with their modular syllabuses based upon SHP, although even here the four modules are assessed through two written papers and coursework. All four English groups also offer SHP syllabuses whose course structure is essentially modular in nature, although not hitherto set out in terms of equal units of instruction.

SYLLABUS CONTENT

As far as content is concerned, the history criteria make no attempt to be prescriptive (Section 4; see Chapter 1, Figure 4), beyond insisting that each examining group must provide at least one syllabus which helps students towards an understanding of the intellectual, cultural, technological and political growth of the United Kingdom, and of the effects of these developments on the lives of its citizens (para. 4.1). No one, however, is *required* to take such a syllabus. There is also an insistence that all syllabuses must describe their content in some detail and that whatever the content it must meet certain broad stipulations relating to coherence, balance, depth and breadth and be capable of dealing with key issues (paras 4.3 and 4.4).

In real terms most examining groups have determined their

syllabus coverage by reference to the current GCE O level and CSE market and have therefore produced syllabuses in modern world history, economic and social history since approximately 1760, and nineteenth- and twentieth-century British and European history. The extent to which this provision will be significantly more varied and perhaps more interesting in the future will depend on two things: first, consumer pressure and, second, and more significant, the extent to which the general criteria stipulations in respect of sex and cultural bias are implemented in practice (para. 19 h and i).

WRITTEN QUESTIONS

In the early years of GCSE both the content of the syllabuses and the overall pattern of assessment (with the exception of 'coursework for all') are unlikely to be very different from much current O level and CSE practice. What ought to be – indeed must be – different if differentiation is to be achieved and the criteria met are the kinds of questions asked both in the formal examination and in coursework, and the ways in which these are marked.

History examining and hence classroom practice has been dominated for decades by two major types of question to which the labels 'short answer' and 'essay' have been attached. The short-answer format can range from the simple, as, for, example, 'Name the battle in which the Russian Navy was defeated in 1905' (by whom, incidentally?) to the more complicated, as, for example, multiple-choice items (which are not being used in GCSE history). The archetypal essay question tends to read something like this: 'Describe the purposes that the OAU was designed to serve.' Both these questions actually appear in the London and East Anglian Group's (LEAG) specimen paper for its Syllabus A, modern world history, but could equally well have appeared in any O level or CSE paper over the past decade. The second example, incidentally, forms the first part of a two-part question. The second part is another equally typical essay question and reads, 'Write an account of the history of the OAU from its foundations to the present day.' It might have been helpful if the full title of the OAU (Organisation of African Unity) and not simply the initials had been used.

The problem is that questions of this type which appear in GCSE specimen papers, and will almost certainly appear in the 1988 first GCSE examination, are deficient in two major respects. First, they fail to differentiate, and, second, they make relatively little contribution to the delivery of the history subject criteria. Why is this? As has been suggested earlier in this chapter, it is partly because of the way in which the questions have been asked, and partly because of the ways in which the answers are likely to be marked. The second ought to result directly from the first, but in practice this doesn't always happen.

Short-answer questions can only be marked on a right/wrong basis, and therefore even if one asks a substantial number of such questions, as is common examination practice, it is only possible to evaluate a student's positive performance by his or her right answers. In such circumstances, the real meaning of a grade A is that those awarded it could not do some 30 per cent of what they were asked to do. This percentage will, of course, vary with the mark at which the grade boundaries are fixed in any given examination. For grade A, this may not matter, but when one reached grade G, the negative nature of the message that these candidates 'did not know' or 'could not do' some 75 per cent of what they were asked to do is all too clear.

Essay questions, on the other hand, often fail to make their requirements clear to those answering them. (There are those, however, who believe that this is one of their advantages!) It is, in consequence, difficult to determine whether answers which are less than adequate have been caused by an inability to understand the question, or by limitations in the necessary skills or understanding required to answer them. The elimination of the first possibility is an essential pre-requisite to the delivery of positive achievement and hence differentiation. Lack of clarity in the questions is moreover a major reason for the widespread use of mark schemes, which arise from the examiner's view of what ought to constitute the 'right' answer, rather than those which arise from the nature and range of answers which the questions are intended to produce. Differentiation which relies on common questions can only result from students' answers and in consequence the questions used must aim to extend the range and possibilities of these answers.

Given the line of argument put forward in the last few paragraphs, there is clearly little that can be done to improve the sample short-answer question except to avoid using it. The same would be true of the second part of the essay question on the OAU, which tests little more than memory and logical presentation. The first part of the essay question could, however, be significantly improved by adding something along the following lines: 'Which do you consider to be the most important? Give reasons for your choice.'

It will be necessary, however, to do rather more than patch up basically deficient questions. What is needed is a model for the setting and marking of questions which will encourage all students to provide evidence of their varying but positive achievements in relation to the skills, concepts and understandings set out in Assessment Objectives 3.2, 3.3 and 3.4, secure in the knowledge that these will all be recognised and rewarded. Such a model already exists if people are willing to use it as a result of the experience of the Schools History Project, whose objectives are virtually identical to the history subject criteria. The next few pages will explore what this model is likely to mean for GCSE examination practice. Although the main focus will be upon the external aspects of assessment, and examples will be provided from the specimen papers of the GCSE groups, the issues raised will be very largely the same as those facing teachers evaluating, as they must, the performance of their own pupils for diagnostic purposes against the criteria.

MODEL FOR DIFFERENTIATED ASSESSMENT

The first major feature of the model is that it makes substantial use of questions centred around key ideas such as the distinction between information and evidence. These questions pose problems, dilemmas or paradoxes. The second feature is that question-setting is based upon careful consideration of what makes a question difficult, and the third is that the model uses a marking methodology based upon levels of response. Although it was designed initially to assess skills involved in handling sources, it is equally appropriate for use in assessing empathy and concepts, although much less work has been undertaken to date in these areas, particularly the latter.

The decision to use problematic, paradoxical or dilemmic questions was an essentially pragmatic response to criteria which stress above all the development of reasoning and thinking skills amongst young people. It has had one very important consequence, namely, that we ought to stop trying to test skills in isolation. Largely due to Bloom, this notion has influenced a great deal of assessment practice in history since the early 1970s. The attempt had led to far too simplistic a view of what a skill such as comprehension actually means, and there is in consequence a need to unpack the term. When this is done, something like the following is likely to emerge.

COMPREHENSION (sources seen as information)
Extract from single source $\longrightarrow$ Extract from more than one source $\longrightarrow$ Cross-refer in terms of positive $\longrightarrow$ negative $\longrightarrow$ null correspondence.

COMPREHENSION (sources seen as evidence)
Advance proposition from a single source $\longrightarrow$ Advance proposition from more than one source $\longrightarrow$ Cross-refer in terms of propositions advanced to show positive $\longrightarrow$ negative $\longrightarrow$ null correspondence.

It is clear that the student who reaches the final stage (cross-reference in terms of null correspondence) will have to exercise skills other than comprehension, for example inference or evaluation. This issue is not quite the same when one is assessing concepts such as causation and change, or assessing empathy. It will still be necessary to unpack the terms here in order to determine what they mean in practice, but this will occur primarily along a single dimension. It would lead in consequence to marking levels which reflect greater understanding of the concept rather than a series of overlapping or interlocking skills.

Structure and Written Questions

Structure or the room for manoeuvre which particular questions pose for candidates has always been a key issue in relation to question-setting. It has, however, assumed a new significance with the requirement in GCSE history to differentiate through common questions. Problems, dilemmas or paradoxes can encourage a wide range of answers, but they can only do this in examinations if the candidates' possible responses are carefully and deliberately controlled.

The first significant use of structuring in public examinations arose from the desire to unpack the format of the traditional essay question in order to try and make it more comprehensible to the less able. Thus, for example, 'Describe and evaluate Britain's role at sea during the First World War' could be turned into a three-part question as follows:

Example 2

(a) Why was Britain concerned about her sea power during the First World War?
(b) What were Britain's main actions in the war at sea between 1914 and 1918?
(c) How successful was Britain in the war at sea between 1914 and 1918?

(Southern Examining Group (SEG) specimen GCSE paper, Syllabus 4, British history, 1815–1983).
(Incidentally, will all students be clear what is meant by 'concerned'?)

It soon became apparent from using questions of this type that making a question easy to comprehend did not of itself necessarily make it any easier to answer. Indeed, unpacking questions in this way might well have made them more difficult because additional questions were now being asked of whose existence the respondents might have been blissfully unaware. This may not be the case in the example above because the three-part question has to some degree broken down the word 'evaluate' which may have caused trouble to some candidates. However, whether the two versions give the students similar messages is open to doubt.

There was also another variant of structuring introduced about the same time which aimed at telling candidates something about the framework the examiner would be using for marking as in the following, for example.

Example 3

'Describe the developments which took place in British industry in the later years of the nineteenth century. Refer in your answers to (a) new products, (b) new sources of power, (c) new modes of transport.'

(London and East Anglian Group (LEAG) specimen paper, finally approved version for GCSE 1988, history Syllabus C.)
(How 'new' is 'new', incidentally?) This particular question was followed by a second part which read

'How far may these developments be described as a second Industrial Revolution?'

It will be noted that both these examples of structuring appear in specimen papers issued by two of the GCSE groups. The extent to which they will, in practice, differentiate must be open to question, but an opportunity will be provided later in the chapter to look at some proposals for marking. It was also considered that structuring might ease the problem of the less-able by limiting the field from which an answer could be drawn. For example, instead of saying, 'Discuss the role of practical and magical forces in early societies,' the question might read,

Example 4

> Many early civilisations saw the world in which they lived as a mixture of practical and magical forces. Choose one early society and answer the following questions.
> (1) What skills did the people of this society have? What machines and/or inventions did they use? (10)
> (2) Describe how these people explained the things which they did not understand. How was their society organised? (15)
> (3) Because these people did not have as much scientific knowledge as we do, does this mean their society could not cope with the problems it faced? (15)

(Northern Ireland Schools Examinations Council (NISEC), history GCSE specimen papers for 1988, final version).

The marks in brackets appear on the question paper, and the examiner will in consequence have to use them, however the question works in practice.

Quite apart from the marking, to which reference will be made later, this question raises a number of significant issues. The first is its length in comparison with the original. One of the problems of structuring is that it is almost impossible to achieve clarity without lengthening the question. This may well create reading problems and hence inhibit access to the question for certain students. Secondly, it must be a matter of some debate as to whether the attempt to restrict the question's scope has made it more or less manageable, or more or less difficult than the original. Does it not simply impose in a more complex form a different range of demands which some may find easier and others more difficult? Finally, there is the use of the paradox in the third part to which the student is invited to respond, rather than being asked to describe or discuss. This has important implications for both teaching and for the evaluation of student responses. It would almost certainly have been better if the whole of the question had been couched in the form of a paradox and, in consequence, greatly shortened. The following example taken from an SHP in-service training exercise illustrates this latter point quite well. It begins with Source A (iii), an illustration showing Hippocrates examining the urine of one of his patients.

Example 5

> Hippocrates was an ancient Greek physician, but in Source A (iii) he is shown wearing European clothes. What does this

61

suggest about the ways in which medieval doctors came to learn about the ideas of Hippocrates?

This question also raises the issue of whether or not profitable use has been made of the illustration. It is all too easy for such material to become mere window-dressing, and clearly this question could have been asked without the illustration if it had been slightly re-worded. Despite this, however, a picture might provide a better stimulus for some students.

If it is one's primary aim in structuring questions to assist the student, then it is necessary to take note of what goes on in the classroom. In particular it is necessary to take note of the kinds of questions which teachers ask their students, and those that students ask themselves and their fellows in order to develop specific skills and concepts. Part of the material in the one-term SHP *What is History?* unit, designed for students around the ages of 13 or 14, relates to an incident in the 1913 Derby, when a suffragette, Emily Davison, threw herself under the King's horse in the Derby and was killed. The principal sources of information regarding this incident are a photograph and a written account, and questions are asked with the aim of encouraging comparisons to be made between the two sources in order to elicit similarities and differences and to account for them. It is clear from classroom observation that the students who come most quickly to terms with this material and its potential utility as evidence are those who ask themselves at an early stage, 'I wonder where the photographer was standing when he or she took the photograph?' Consideration of this question (to which a correct answer is impossible to determine) is crucial to an understanding of how Emily Davison managed to do what she did. A number of students never ask themselves this question – nor incidentally do some teachers – whilst others arrive at it very slowly and after considerable help.

It would however be possible to build in such questions as the first part of an examination question, not with the intention of awarding them marks, although it may be necessary to give one or two, but of helping the students to look at issues which they might otherwise have ignored. Such 'feeder' questions, as they have come to be called, thus make it more likely that more students will be able to get to grips with the main question or questions at issue – an important prerequisite for differentiation through common questions.

An illustration of such a feeder question in a GCSE specimen paper is provided by the first part of the following question, which is simply intended to indicate to the candidates the important part played by the microscope in the development of germ theory.

Example 6

The germ theory of diseases was developed in the late nineteenth century in Europe by Pasteur, Koch and others.
(a) How did improvements in microscopes help to make this possible? (2 marks)
(b) What other factors also helped to bring about the germ theory? Briefly explain how each factor you mentioned helped in this. (8 marks)
(c) What was the importance of the germ theory in the history of medicine? (10 marks)

(SEG, SHP, GCSE Examination. Specimen Paper 1, medicine.)

You will note how small a weighting this first part attracts by comparison with the other two parts.

Another basis for structuring is to make use of students' misconceptions as part of the question framework. Students tend, for example, to regard photographs as inherently more reliable than other sources because the former are 'scientific'! Similarly, primary sources are thought to be more reliable than secondary sources simply because they are primary, or because those responsible for them were there! One needs deliberately to challenge these misconceptions as part of the questioning process. Similarly, accuracy is often seen as a prerequisite for establishing source reliability. This misconception is challenged in the following question. (Sources (h) and (i) are pictures of skeletons dancing.)

Example 7

The pictures shown in sources (h) and (i) are imaginery – skeletons do not dance! Does this make (h) and (i) unreliable as sources of evidence? Explain your answer.

(SEG, SHP, GCSE Examination Paper 2.)

Work over the past five years on structuring questions along lines such as those suggested in the past few paragraphs has led to a development of a framework which takes account of the various ways in which questions can be made both more or less accessible and more or less difficult. There is a relationship between the two, although it is not a straight-line one. Difficulty can be introduced into a question along one or more of four dimensions, as illustrated in Figure 1. These four dimensions can be altered to some degree independently of each other, though there is inevitably a close relationship between, say, the period studied in history and its associated sources.

The ease or difficulty of a question can thus be altered in a variety of different ways. For example, some sources are harder to make sense of than others. Inference may be harder than comprehension (on the other hand, it may not). Objective items make different demands from essay questions, and so on. Ideally, one ought to retain the principal difficulty of any question within the conceptual/skill dimension and avoid making the other dimensions gratuitously difficult. This, however, will always remain a counsel of perfection since the sources, the content, the skills, the concepts and the format all need to be knitted into a unified whole. What both the classroom

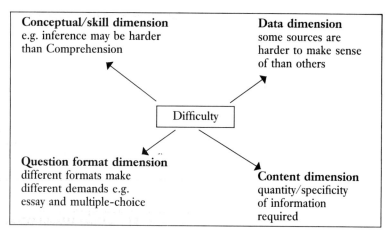

▲ *Fig. 1*

teacher and the GCSE examiner can do with advantage is to use the ideas contained in the framework to suggest a list of questions that need to be asked of questions. For example,

a) What kinds of responses do I anticipate from this question? (What kind of skills or ideas is it addressing?)
b) Can anticipated answers be ordered along a single, conceptual or skill dimension, or not? (Will the question test one thing or many, and which do I intend it should test?)
c) Of the sorts of responses anticipated, how many merit award? What is the lowest rewardable response? (Will the question differentiate in terms of the concept/skill mastery with which I am concerned?)
d) Is the question primarily intended to assist the student or to help the examiner?
e) How many words could be eliminated without changing the sense of the question?
f) How many 'difficult' words could be replaced with 'easier' ones without changing the sense of the question?

The aim in asking these questions would be to improve or replace questions with others that did the same job more effectively. Clearly, it is not possible to expose every question one asks in the classroom to this kind of shredding process. But classroom practice would improve significantly if such an exercise was undertaken on a regular basis. For those setting examinations such a process should become a routine.

In constructing questions it is also important to ensure that their wording encourages those answering them to use the kinds of skills or undertake the kinds of thinking which will enable them to address the problems with which they are confronted and hence show their qualities. Words such as 'discuss' or 'describe' rarely do this. John Fines in his pamphlet on source-based questions at GCE A level, published by the Historical Association, has an extremely useful list of question formats relating to handling, evaluating and applying sources which will repay careful study. It will have been noted that some of the questions in the list provided in the previous paragraph contain references to marking and this question will be addressed later in the chapter.

What kinds of questions are likely to result from this approach to question-setting, and to what extent will they be found in the GCSE in 1988? This can best be answered by providing some examples, the first of which is to be found in Chapter 2, and the others come from GCSE specimen papers prepared by the examining groups. The question (Example G) on page 32 on the Munich Agreement provides a good illustration of a structured question based upon sources which poses a paradox, as does Example H on First World War propaganda. These are teaching questions and might need some reorganisation for use in an examination, but essentially they are trying to do in the classroom what the examination also has to do, namely to test the criteria in ways which are accessible to all students and thus enable them all to show what they know, understand and can do. If successful in the classroom over the full ability range then they should be equally successful in an examination, although inevitably time constraints will play a greater part in the latter than in the former. The one fundamental difference lies in the marking. Teachers will be concerned to obtain information which they can use for diagnostic purposes; to look, for example, at the problems faced by a particular individual or the way they have taught a particular topic. The examiner's prime concern is to award grades and, however comprehensive and thoughtful the marking procedures are, it will be necessary at some stage to make distinctions in performance for that purpose.

Regrettably, there are not many good examples of similar questions to be found in the GCSE specimen papers, though there are plenty of earlier and less well developed forms of structuring. Moreover, the overwhelming majority of the 'best' questions to be found in the specimen papers occur within the SHP syllabuses, whose lessons do not appear to have been learnt fully by those setting examinations upon other syllabuses. The result will inevitably be inadequate differentiation, and this will not be in the best interests of students at the ends of the ability range.

The following five questions would appear to illustrate quite well many of the suggestions made earlier in this chapter. The reader might like to ask them some of the questions posed on page 64 about questions, particularly the last two. The reader might also wish to consider the extent to which these sample questions are likely to differentiate over the full GCSE ability range in the light of the points made earlier in the chapter. The first three questions (Examples 8–10) assume that the candidates will have studied the period to which the questions refer, and they will therefore be expected to use the knowledge and understanding gained from this study in answering the questions. The fourth question (Example 11) is based entirely upon given sources, although the candidates will have studied the topic as part of their course. Where marks appear in brackets, this means they also appear on the question papers.

Example 8

What are the advantages and disadvantages for a historian of the Middle East in using the following sources as evidence?
(a) The memoirs of a politician who was involved in events such as Sources A and C. (6)
(b) Cartoons as in Source B. (4)

(Midlands Examining Group (MEG) History, the Modern World 1914 to the present day, 1988 specimen question papers for the GCSE.)

(Sources A and C consist of an extract from Chaim Herzog's *The Arab – Israeli Wars* and from Nasser quoted in *The Middle East* by Richard Lawless, 1980. Source B is a single cartoon. The sources are not reproduced in full here, since the question intends that they should be used merely as illustrations in order to address a general problem.)

Example 9

'Now, Custer, don't be greedy, wait for us.' General Gibbon at the briefing before the march to Little Bighorn. 'No, I won't.' Custer's reply.
(a) Why did General Gibbon want Custer to wait before attacking the Sioux? (4 marks)
(b) General Terry, who was in overall command of the expedition, said that if Custer had waited for Gibbon the Indians would have been defeated. Do you think we should believe Terry? Explain your answer. (6 marks)
(c) Was the defeat of Custer at Little Bighorn really a victory for the Indians? Explain your answer. (10 marks)

(SEG, SHP, 1988 GCSE Examination, specimen questions, the American West.)

Example 10

In what ways did the coming of the railways affect the lives of people living in Victorian times? How does this compare with the effect of modern road transport on people living in the twentieth century?

(Northern Examining Association (NEA) GCSE specimen paper, history Syllabus C, British – Economic and Social.)

Example 11

Read the two sources below carefully and then answer the questions which follow.

Source A
'On the 12th July 1588, the Great Armada set sail from Spain. The huge ships under the Duke of Medina Sidonia were like floating sea-castles. But they were much less dangerous than they looked. England had only thirty vessels of war, but they were very new and efficient. The Spanish fleet consisted of one

hundred and thirty vessels which were well manned. There were more Spanish soldiers waiting in the Netherlands under the command of the Duke of Parma. The plan was for the Armada to link up with the forces in the Netherlands. The Spanish ships would then land their armies in England and conquer it for the Spanish king.

The English fleet put out to sea, missed the Spaniards, but turned and hurried them up the Channel. The Armada put into Calais harbour. The English sent fire ships drifting among the fleet, throwing it into confusion and destroying many of the ships. Next day the Armada sailed North. The Spaniards missed Parma who was waiting in the Netherlands with his army. Then a strong wind drove the Spanish ships into confusion up the North Sea.

Storm tossed, the Armada drifted on. Some ships were wrecked off the Shetland Islands. Others struggled on to Ireland only to be wrecked on the coast there. The Armada was a failure. Not a single Spanish sailor landed in this country. Only fifty-three ships of the great fleet got home to Spain. The Armada failed because the English adopted a new method of fighting and the Spanish method was too old fashioned to stand against it.'

Source B
'The Armada came out of Corunna and took course for the North. But tempests obliged it to take refuge on the coast of France. From there the Duke of Medina Sidonia foolishly sailed out, ignoring the advice of his best sailors. The heavy Spanish ships were then prey to the light English boats, which were able to attack and approach more efficiently. The undeniable skill of the pirate Drake saved England from a real disaster.

A terrible wind from the south east was disturbing the sea. The rain began in a flood. The hurricanes beat upon the ships scattering them, then sending them crashing together.

The invincible Armada was for the first time conquered – but not by men. It was defeated by the weather. Only against the hurricane and the gales did we lose, because God wished it.'

(a) What does Source A suggest was the Spanish plan for invading Spain? (2)
(b) Give two reasons put forward in Source A for the defeat of the Spanish Armada. (4)
(c) What does Source B suggest about the main reason for the Armada's defeat? (4)
(d) Which source do you think was written by (i) an Englishman, (ii) a Spaniard? Explain your choice briefly. (2)
(e) Give an example of any biased language you can detect in each source. (6)
(f) Do you think either one of these sources can be considered more truthful than the other? Give reasons for your answer. (7)

(Welsh Joint Education Committee (WJEC) GCSE History Syllabus A – Modular. Specimen question paper.)

Note the significant difference here between the first three questions which test simple reading comprehension and are unlikely to differentiate, and the last three which are much more demanding. In this connection it is worth asking whether the marks awarded for question (d) are not too low.

Example 12

'The Korean War achieved nothing. By the end of it both sides were back where they started.' Explain fully whether or not you agree with this statement. (15 marks)

(MEG, History, the Modern World, 1914 to the Present Day, 1988 GCSE specimen question papers.)

This constituted the third of a series of questions upon the Korean War which had one piece of supporting material consisting of two maps of Korea at different times in the 1950s. These were directly used in the first two questions, which together counted for 10 marks out of a total of 25.

EMPATHY

There has been relatively little specific reference to empathy so far in this chapter, largely because the issues relating to it have been substantially addressed in the previous chapter. This has provided a number of useful classroom questions and these, as with the majority of the questions in Chapter 2, could be used with minor modifications in an examination. They also illustrate quite well that the framework proposed earlier for question-setting is equally valid for assessing empathy, or the ability to look at events and issues from the perspective of people in the past, as criterion 3.3 puts it. It would probably be fair to say that the substantial work undertaken on teaching and assessing empathy in recent years has resulted in a slightly more utilitarian view being taken of it as a tool to illuminate motivation and to extend the record when the existing sources are inadequate, as in pre-history. This has to some degree downgraded the emphasis placed upon imagination, which was once central, since we now recognise that however hard we try we cannot stand in someone else's shoes. Our resulting search for greater knowledge about particular pairs of shoes, and our concern to judge the behaviour of those standing in them, must not, however, blind us to the enduring significance for history of a good story well told, whether in writing or orally, or in drama, or in simulation. It is this that makes people in the past come alive and cease to be cardboard cut-outs – an essential starting point for developing empathy.

This more utilitarian approach has shown itself in assessment terms in the significant reduction of the once popular 'imagine you are' questions, although there are a few survivors in the GCSE specimen papers.

Example 13

In Nuremberg in 1946 an international tribunal assembled to try prominent remaining Nazis. Write
(a) an opening speech by the Chief Prosecutor, detailing the crimes of the Nazi regime between 1933 and 1939.

(b) A statement by one of the accused defending himself against such charges.

(WJEC, GCSE History, Syllabus A – Modular. Specimen question paper.)

Much more common, however, are questions or parts of questions which are designed to assess such things as using sources as a basis for understanding contemporary attitudes, or which offers the possibility of an empathetic explanation alongside explanations based on knowledge, or common sense. Sometimes these questions are very directive; on other occasions they are more problem-orientated in their approach.

Example 14

How do sources A and B together help us to understand attitudes towards the education of the poor at that time?
(4 marks)

(MEG, GCSE history, British social and economic history, 1988 specimen question papers.)

Sources A and B consist of two pictures of a mid-nineteenth-century power loom factory, and a mid-nineteenth-century monitorial school. The question, although free-standing, forms part of a series of six based upon four sources, the two pictures and two written sources, which together are worth a total of 30 marks.

Example 15

The Swing Rioters were complaining about unemployment and very low wages, yet they destroyed the farms on which they might have worked. How can you explain this? (10 marks)

This is the third part of a series of questions on the Swing Riots, counting for 20 marks, which did not use any sources.

(SEG, GCSE, SHP 1988, specimen Britain 1815–51.)

Example 16

When people like those shown in Source G were not cured, they often followed the King around, being touched over and over again. Why did people living in the Middle Ages still believe in cures like this, even if they did not work?

(SEG, GCSE, SHP 1988, specimen Medicine)

Source G is a picture from a thirteenth-century manuscript showing Edward the Confessor touching for 'scrofula'. It is the third of a series of four questions based upon three sources (two written, one picture) which together count for 40 marks.

The WJEC question above is likely to produce a greater use of imagination, but on the evidence to date much of this is likely to be mis-directed. The MEG question, on the other hand, is likely to produce answers which will reveal greater understanding of contemporary attitudes, but may well not encourage the use of imagination. Do the SEG questions provide a middle road which will still encourage the use of imagination, but a use disciplined by its context and a need for a solid and accurate information? Above all, do the four questions differentiate? Readers will have to judge this for themselves, and to help them in this some of the marking schemes proposed by the groups will subsequently be looked at.

MARKING PROCEDURES

It is of no use whatsoever setting interesting questions or papers which encourage a wide range of positive responses, if the marking procedures cannot reward these answers validly and reliably in accordance with the requirements of the subject criteria. The vital importance of devising appropriate mark schemes was recognised very early in the life of SHP, with particular reference to the use of unseen sources in Paper 2. It was not however until 1978 that a scheme based upon the allocation of marks for criteria was used. Initially, tentative hierarchies of criteria based upon progressive levels of abstraction were developed for each question prior to the examination as a result of discussion and informal trialling. These were constructed by identifying what was to count as a baseline answer to the question under consideration and then working upwards. An example of such a hierarchy (which, it must be stressed, is only applicable to a single specific question) is as follows:

Level 1. Ability to relate conclusions to sources supplied.
Level 2. Ability to ask specific questions of sources.
Level 3. Ability to make simple generalisations on the basis of evidence.
Level 4. Ability to extend an account by cross-referencing between sources ...

Level N. Ability to consider what is to count as sufficiency of evidence.

The gap between level 4 and level N, which was considered to be the ultimate criterion in this set applicable to 14–16-year-olds, indicates that there are other levels which could be measured. Subsequent investigation in fact suggested another three. It would be an interesting, but fruitless, exercise to set a question to which a marking scheme based on these levels could be applied. It would be fruitless, because the starting point for developing such mark schemes is the setting of the questions. There is widespread, indeed almost universal, use of levels in the marks scheme in the GCSE specimen papers for history, as reference to the syllabuses of the five groups will show. Many of these will not, however, work satisfactorily because they have been imposed subsequently upon questions which will not generate a satisfactory range of answers within manageable dimensions, instead of flowing naturally from the intentions of the question. The message is stark: marking levels can only emerge from questions. They cannot create or improve questions.

The starting point for setting questions, therefore, must be to answer the first question which appeared on the list on page 64, namely, What kinds of responses do we anticipate from it? This will provide a range of possible targets for the question which can subsequently be reduced or expanded in the light of discussion and pre-test evidence. Some questions, particularly those intended to assess concepts, will concentrate upon a single target, for example understanding of causation or awareness of cause/consequence.

The challenge here to the question-setter is to construct questions which, through a combination of data, content and format, will produce answers from all students across the levels deemed appropriate for an understanding of the concept. In the case of awareness of cause/consequence, these might range from a single mono-causal response at level 1 through answers which considered both long- and short-term consequences to a fully balanced answer which in the case of a question, say, upon the Second World War, might show an awareness of the complexity of causation and that the build-up to any major event takes place over a long period. The number of levels will of course depend upon the opportunities which any particular question provides. Empathetic questions, unless they form part of questions designed to explore motivation, will try to provide opportunities for students to demonstrate their capacity in relation to the stages described on pages 25–6 of Chapter 2. The starting point or lowest level would be 'everyday empathy' and the highest 'differentiated historical empathy'. At every stage, relevant, factual information would improve the quality of the answers, but would not change the level of the response.

Other questions, particularly those making use of sources, could either provide the student with a range of targets, as for example 'motivation and interpretation of sources', or 'motivation, empathy and hypothesis formation', or they could concentrate upon a single target such as 'anachronism' or 'evaluating within the context'. The main problem when using a range of targets (and this will almost inevitably occur when the question itself poses a problem or confronts candidates with a dilemma, or paradox) lies in the ordering of the levels, which for marking purposes have to be hierarchical in nature. It must be recognised that this, like the majority of decisions relating to marking in public examination, involves subjective judgements, but these can and must be tempered by setting procedures that involve substantial pre-testing.

The process of developing the 'levels' mark scheme which is actually used in the examination takes time and trouble. The initial tentative marking criteria should be trialled, along with the questions, upon a representative sample and then adjusted in the light of what the pre-test has to say. Some levels will be collapsed and others added. The issue of manageability also needs to be borne in mind. How many levels can examiners actually hold in their minds at once? This needs to be balanced against the fineness of the distinctions one needs or wishes to make between students. SHP has used pre-testing to develop a range of in-service training material which, quite apart from its general use for teachers, forms a key element in the training of new examiners. Instead of being asked to give a mark to an answer, the examiners are asked to identify the highest criterion or level achieved in each answer. Originally, no marks were awarded at all, but subsequently a notional mark has been assigned to each question and a small band of marks allocated to each level. The reasons for this are two-fold: first, because examiners find it difficult not to use marks and, secondly, to permit distinctions in quality to be made within a single level. Thus the awarding of marks, although governed by the criterial level of the responses, is flexible enough to accommodate a personal appraisal of quality by an examiner.

So much for the generalities. How do such mark schemes actually operate in practice? This can best be illustrated by setting down the levels proposed by the groups from marking a selection of the specimen questions provided earlier in the chapter. Those chosen are Examples 2, 6, 10, 14 and 16. The interested reader can find the mark schemes for the remaining questions with the specimen question papers published by the relevant group. The mark schemes will simply be printed as published and will be followed by a brief comment.

Mark scheme for Example 2 (page 60)

(a) **Level 1.** Narrative answers: candidates simply say what was happening at the time; 1–3.

Level 2. Single-factor explanation. Candidates pick out one factor only; 4–6.

Level 3. Multi-factor explanation. Candidates pick out more than one factor, but do not make links between them; 7–9.

Level 4. Web of motivation answers. Candidates make links between various factors; 10–12.

(b) Award two marks for each correct action; maximum 8 marks.

(c) **Level 1.** Narrative; 1–3.

Level 2. Answers supported by generalised recall; 4–7.

Level 3. Answers supported by specific recall; 8–10.

TOTAL: 30 marks.

This scheme illustrates the problem of using 'levels' marking with questions which largely test recall. It is doubtful, moreover, whether part (a) as worded will generate the kinds of answers assumed by the levels.

Mark scheme for Example 6 (page 63)

(a) 1 mark per precise point in brief explanation; 2 marks.

(b) **Level 1.** Able to choose valid factor, but no worthwhile explanation; maximum 3 marks.

Level 2. As level 1, but supports choice with relevant precise detail; maximum 6 marks.

Level 3. As level 1, but explains how factor led to the germ theory; maximum 8 marks.

(c) **Level 1.** Naive view of importance within medical technology; 1 mark.

Level 2. More sophisticated view, but still confined to technical results; 2–5 marks.

Level 3. *Historical* importance assured; 5–10 marks.

TOTAL: 20 marks.

Are these distinctions sufficient to enable reliable marking to take place, bearing in mind that the marks scheme will provide illustrations of answers which fall into each level?

Mark scheme for Example 10 (page 66)

The NEA proposes a single framework for marking essays, of which this is one. No mark bands are provided. The framework is as follows:

Level 1. A largely factual account, with some disconnected ideas. When ideas appear they will tend to be generalised or narrowly based. Factual content will usually be relevant, but not necessarily comprehensive.

Level 2. A factually orientated account with some attempt at explanation or analysis. The candidate can demonstrate a general overall view of the problem set, the handling of which will usually be straightforward, avoiding or simplifying complications.

Level 3. A descriptive and analytical account clearly addressing the question set, in which the candidate is able to relate factual knowledge to points of analysis, to propose problems and solve them at a simple level and to find solutions to the problems posed by the question.

Level 4. An account in which the material is used in a sophisticated and purposeful way to illustrate the writer's ideas: the analytical content now tending to provide the dominant framework for the answers. The candidate displays an awareness of historical problem, is alert to and, where appropriate, can offer more than one interpretation of them.

The target for the questions will normally be the testing of assessment objectives (a) and (b). These are (a) recall, evaluate and select knowledge relevant to the context and display it in clear and coherent form, (b) understand and make use of the concepts of cause and consequence, continuity and change, similarity and difference. The framework will serve as a basis for each marking scheme and may be more finely tuned for any one specific question.

Are the general levels described above realistic, or is the scheme simply using the notion of levels to provide useful general advice? What would a finely tuned scheme for marking Example 10 actually look like? Is the question, particularly the last part, likely to differentiate?

Mark scheme for Example 14 (page 69)

Level 1. Gives a general answer which does not refer to sources about attitudes to the education of the poor. (1 mark)

Level 2. Looks at one source only, probably B, and uses it to explain attitudes towards the education of the poor, e.g. large numbers together, use of monitors who knew little more than their charges (2–3 marks).

Level 3. Sees correlation between the pictures and such ideas as mass production reflected in the education of the masses; perhaps even appreciates the utilitarian attitude (4 marks).

This scheme appears to make a realistic and differentiated breakdown of the levels of answers that the question is likely to generate, but the marks awarded appear far too small and restricted to make genuine distinctions between possible answers. Should not the last phrase in level 3 constitute a possible level 4?

Mark scheme for Example 16 (page 69)

Level 1. Explanation from the outside. Reference to concrete historical factors. Believed in supernatural cures because lived in a religious age. (1–3 marks)

Level 2. Explanation from the inside. Everyday empathy, because genuine attempt to show royal touch could have seemed reasonable to people at the time, but reconstruction remains locked in twentieth-century world view. No attempt to recreate an alien form of life, or way of thinking, i.e. 'people desperate and had nothing to lose, because no alternative recourse'. (4–6 marks)

Level 3. Explanation from the outside – historical empathy. Attempt to show how belief in royal touch was reasonable to the medieval mind. Genuine attempt to shed twentieth-century preconceptions and to recreate alien world view. Disease the reward of sin; cure signals forgiveness; forgiveness must be merited; following King around may be thought of as a penance. (7–10 marks)

Here the 'levels' marks scheme appears to provide a genuine match between what the question requires and the answers it is likely to generate. The provision of illustrative answers is also helpful.

It is to be hoped that these illustrations will have provided greater insight to the notions underlying 'levels' marks schemes. Such schemes are likely to be particularly helpful to teachers for diagnostic use. It also seems likely that the examining groups will agree to publish a GCSE marking scheme, and this will be to everyone's benefit as well as helping to create a much more open environment.

WEIGHTING

Reference has been made from time to time to the weighting of questions, and it will be noted that virtually all the sample questions provided as illustrations indicated the marks to be awarded on the question paper itself—a decision with which the examiners will have to live, however the question works in practice. This procedure must be questionable, given the requirement to differentiate across a range of criteria by means of common questions. In particular, it raises two issues: first, question choice and, second, *post hoc* weighting. In the longer term, successful differentiation in relation to a range of skills and concepts can only be achieved by the diminution of choice within written examinations and the use of weighting which is based upon actual and not upon anticipated answers. Pre-testing makes it possible to narrow the gap between anticipated and actual levels of performance, but it still remains far too wide for comfort, and the capacity for correction and adjustment within mark schemes remains essential.

A solution has been devised for this problem by SHP which has been given the name of *post hoc* weighting. It makes use of marks as a convenience and, at the marking stage there is therefore no indication of the final weighting which any question will carry. This weighting is subsequently achieved by:

a) Establishing those question levels which have in practice been reached by significant numbers of candidates in the actual examination. What constitutes 'significant' will have to be agreed in advance.
b) Constructing a paper level scale, that is to say a description not of what a paper was intended to test, but what it actually did test in any given year in the light of the candidates' actual answers.
c) Relating question levels to equivalent paper levels. When *post hoc* weighting is used, it is not of course possible to allow question choice. In other words, all candidates have to answer all questions.

Reduction in question choice is likely indeed to be an increasingly significant feature of the GCSE, particularly as our ideas regarding question setting and differentiation develop. In any case, the placing of marks on question papers, which tends to be an indirect result of choice, places a severe and quite unwarranted strain on examiners. The elimination of marks on question papers will, however, require consideration to be given to alternative ways of advising candidates as to how to use their time most profitably. Various methods are currently being looked at, from starring questions to an indication of length of answer, but none is wholly satisfactory.

This is not the place to provide further detail about the *post hoc* weighting scheme, but there are already clear signs in the proposals emanating from the groups that the whole question of *post hoc* weighting will need to be addressed as greater experience develops in the use of setting and marking procedures designed to achieve differentiation through common questions. Such moves are moreover essential if there is any serious intention to introduce grade criteria operationally into the GCSE. Such schemes have the additional merit of providing teachers with much more information about their candidates' performance for diagnostic use. If the shift implicit in GCSE towards criterion referencing does not help the teacher, then it is not worth pursuing. Those interested in learning more about *post hoc* weighting and the development of paper level scales should obtain copies of the annual examiners reports published by the Southern Regional Examinations Board in respect of the inter-board CSE SHP examinations. A brief account of the process also appears in a contribution by the author to *The History Curriculum for Teachers*, edited by Christopher Portal, Falmer Press, 1987.

It is, of course, not possible in a book of this length to refer to, let alone cover adequately, all relevant issues. There are, however, three topics which have not so far been directly covered, which require mentioning. Namely, the 'in context', 'out of context' debate, reading time and bias. The detail now provided is in no way commensurate with the importance of the topics.

IN CONTEXT – OUT OF CONTEXT

The reader will have seen in the sample questions provided some which require the candidates to supply the context from their own outside knowledge and reading, either with or without supplied material, and others which provide the candidate with the context in the shape of source materials. It is clear that, when additional information has to be supplied, more potentially searching questions can be asked and more wide-ranging answers can be expected, although this is not always the case in practice.

It may, however, be desirable (particularly when differentiating, as in GCSE history through common questions) to use a 'closed set' model of assessment in which all the information needed to answer a question is given to the candidates as part of the question. In this way, a stable common base is provided for comparisons, particularly in the more artificial environment of the written paper. Such an approach will also discourage question-spotting, and it is interesting to note that the history criteria come out strongly against the use of prescribed documents, which represent another potential approach to such spotting (Section 5, Note II).

It is important, however, to ensure that where all the material is supplied the questions asked do not degenerate into a reading comprehension exercise or intelligence tests. The MEG specimen question (Example 8, page 66) illustrates one way of avoiding this. Having supplied the student with the context in the form of two written sources and a cartoon, it follows some questions based upon the sources with a request to evaluate the advantages and disadvantages for the historian of cartoons and written accounts of a similar kind. The candidates are thus compelled to generalise. Similar types or question can be found in the CSE and GCE SHP unseen source papers, which are the most extreme form of closed-set assessment in current use. It is difficult at this stage to come down firmly on one side or the other on this issue, largely because we know too little about young people's capacity to transfer skills learnt in one context to another. What is clear, however, is that teachers must always use sources in context and do all they can to ensure that their students can cope with the widest possible variety of circumstances.

READING TIME

Given the wide ability range for which GCSE is intended, it is obvious that the language level of the sources as well as that of the questions will be crucial in relation to widening access and hence enhancing differentiation. Evidence from SHP has offered two important suggestions here, which the GCSE needs to take on board. First, that the intrinsic interest of both question and material can significantly improve the desire to understand, and hence to read, and, secondly, that prescriptive examination rubrics regarding the necessity to read the sources before answering the questions do little to change candidates normal strategies. What is needed is, first, to build reading time into the overall timing of the examination, and here, as with much else, pre-testing is crucial, and, second, to ensure that the questions set on any group of sources make use of all the material as early as possible, thus ensuring that everything is read.

BIAS

As was mentioned earlier in the chapter, the requirement to avoid bias, both sex and cultural, is written into the *General Criteria* (para. 19 h and i); relatively little, however, has yet been done to find out what this will mean in practice. The GCSE criteria for history, with their emphasis on looking at events and issues from the perspective of people in the past, on the use of sources and on the distinction between information and evidence, can make a powerful contribution to reducing bias. History as a subject, however, can easily and often from the best of motives contribute to bias. One only has to look at the cross-national studies undertaken in recent years upon school textbooks to appreciate this. It is very important, therefore, that both teacher and examiner do not ask questions or pose problems that put particular pupils at a disadvantage. It would be of no help however to anyone if we replace one bias with another, and this is what will inevitably happen if we do not ensure that GCSE examinations are as even-handed as possible for all who wish to take them. Much work needs to be done before we can say that this position has been reached.

COURSEWORK

As Chapter 1 has made clear, an element of coursework counting for at least 20 per cent will form part of the basis for assessment in history for every student who is in full-time education taking the subject. Chapter 2 has provided useful practical advice on the preparation of coursework which has implications for both assessment and teaching. Coursework, it needs to be stressed, is not a form of assessment, but simply work done during a course which can be assessed by any appropriate means. Largely as a result of its having been confined to CSE, a whole series of myths have developed about coursework. Basically, these are saying that coursework is acceptable for the less-able but is inappropriate, even damaging, for the able, that it is time-consuming for both teacher and student and that its marking cannot be reliable because it involves teachers. Moreover the coursework model for history when the groups started to develop their syllabuses was an extremely restricted one, with the main emphasis being placed upon a single finished piece of work known as a project.

In recent years, steps have been taken to improve projects by looking at the possibilities of assessing them by means of an oral, by replacing one big set piece with two smaller set pieces, by allowing more time and the like. But basically, the model has remained the same and this has been matched by a largely inspectorial moderation system in conjunction with initial teacher marking under examining board instructions.

In history, only SHP has broken out of this mould by using a series of small-scale exercises, some five to seven designed to meet quite specific criteria, although even here the stress has remained upon a finished product. SHP has also tended to make use of cluster group or consensus moderation, which has much greater inservice value. Such small-scale exercises or assignments have a number of significant advantages.

1. They require careful whole-course planning and hence facilitate the use of assessment for diagnostic purposes.
2. They can make very specific demands upon students and in consequence can be extremely practical.
3. They lend themselves to and indeed encourage group work.

4. They encourage cross-curricular developments.
5. They can be designed to meet specific individual student interests and hence involve them more directly in both their own learning and their own assessment.
6. They encourage progression and lend themselves particularly well to the demonstration of positive achievement.

With these kinds of advantages, well-planned coursework can make a significant contribution to the achievement of differentiation through the use of different tasks designed to meet the same criteria. For this to be realised in practice two general shifts need to occur: first, a move from one exercise to several, and, second, a move from an emphasis upon product to an emphasis upon process.

The process/product distinction has exercised assessment for a long time. As used in this context, product has meant the finished article, whatever that might be, and the process or more accurately processes are the means whereby the finished product has been produced; the planning and the skills used in the making, and so on. These processes have, however, largely been assessed as if they were products. What is now needed, if certain of the criteria are to be met adequately, is a greater concern with the learning processes as processes and these are, of course, much more difficult to assess, since it is no longer possible to infer and evaluate the process from the product. This will require assessment of the processes in action and will involve much more emphasis on informal observational assessment spread throughout a course, a greater willingness to recognise and report on differences rather than similarities, and a concern for the widest possible spectrum of educational outcomes.

Given history's previous track record in relation to examining coursework, one would not expect to find anything particularly innovative in the GCSE coursework proposals and one would certainly not be disappointed. Outside the SHP syllabuses (and it is curious once again that there appears to be no spin-off from the SHP experience upon other syllabuses, despite the fact that all groups have produced SHP syllabuses), there remains an emphasis on continuous writing, on finished products with word counts and certificates stating that it is the candidate's unaided work, and on inspectorial or statistical moderation, rather than moderation by consensus, which is the only possible way to deal with process-based coursework. Once again it is differentiation that will suffer, and few of the present proposals will allow students to demonstrate positive achievement.

There are, however, signs that this situation will soon change, largely in response to a range of practical problems, rather than to re-thinking of the issues. The first of these is student overload, and the second is the logistics of moderation. The volume of coursework facing a single student taking, say, six to eight GCSE subjects could be enormous, and this has raised the possibility of planning coursework jointly for more than one subject, thus permitting integrated programmes to be developed, say, on a faculty basis. It has also raised the question of what might constitute the minimum evidence needed to make 'fair' judgements about candidates' performance. A similar logistical problem faces the examining groups over moderation, and this has led to serious consideration being given to teacher accreditation, which would enable individual teachers to undertake their own assessment, and hence to plan individual coursework programmes which met the criteria.

Taken together, these issues which incidentally will not go away, serve to underline the irrelevance of much of the current case law concerning coursework and hence may well lead to substantial changes in attitudes over the next few years. What is needed, as Chapter 2 has stressed, is whole-course planning which will integrate coursework and its assessment, whether formal or informal, terminal or in course with teaching and learning. This is after all what Sir Keith Joseph had in mind when he 'invented' criteria and made them the foundation upon which GCSE was based.

As part of the Phase III and IV in-service training provision, and as an aid for encouraging some medium-term thinking about coursework, the Southern Examining Group (SEG) has prepared what it rather grandly called a Coursework Analysis Instrument. A copy of this is attached as an appendix to this chapter (Appendix A) and the reader might care to subject his or her own coursework proposals to its questions.

CONCLUSION

Changes in education, particularly those involving assessment, are inevitably evolutionary in nature. But it will, we hope, be clear from this chapter that there is much still to be done in relation to the assessment of GCSE history if there is not to be a mismatch between the criteria and their delivery through assessment, and between classroom and examination practice. On the evidence of the specimen question papers, few history syllabuses outside SHP are currently delivering positive achievement through common assessment and, hence, are failing to differentiate. This could just be acceptable for 1988, given the pressures faced by all involved, but it will certainly not be acceptable thereafter.

Appendix A — Coursework Analysis Instrument

1 DESIGN

1a Are you going to use projects or structured assignments?
If projects go to 2a if structured assignments go to 2b.

2 DIFFERENTIATION

2a Will all pupils attempt the same type of project, or will tasks be graded by difficulty?
If the same go to 2d if graded by difficulty go to 2b.

2b How will you decide which level of difficulty each candidate will attempt?
If you are satisfied with your answers go to 2c.
If you are not satisfied with your answer reconsider 2a.

2c Can you explain clearly for the moderator what makes certain projects harder than others?
If you are not satisfied with your answer reconsider 2a.
If you are satisfied with your answer go to 2d.

2d How will project titles be arrived at?
Free choice 2e   negotiation 2f   selected from list provided by teacher 2f   single topic which all attempt 2g

2e Access to the right material, and the ease of use of that material, may make some topics harder than others. How will you stop some candidates disadvantaging themselves by choice of topic?
If you are satisfied with your answer go to 2f.
If you are not satisfied with your answer reconsider 2d.

2f Have you got access to the range of sources pupils will need?
If you are satisfied with your answer go to 2k.
If you are not satisfied with your answer reconsider 2d or 1a.

2g Will you need to stop collaboration between pupils or is such collaboration desirable? If it is not desirable how will you guard against it?
If you are satisfied with your answer go to 2f.
If you are not satisfied with your answer reconsider 2d.

2h Will all pupils attempt the same type of exercise, or will exercises be graded by difficulty?
If the same go to 2k if graded by difficulty go to 2i.

2i How will you decide which level of difficulty each candidate will attempt?
If you are satisfied with your answer go to 2j.
If you are not satisfied with your answer reconsider 2b.

2j Can you explain clearly for the moderator what makes certain exercises harder then others?
If you are not satisfied with your answer reconsider 2b.
If you are satisfied with your answer go to 2l.

OTHER ISSUES OF COURSEWORK DESIGN

2k A common problem with essay and project style coursework schemes is that pupils underperform because they do not understand exactly what to do. If you want work on Mary Queen of Scots as a threat to Elizabeth you do not want long descriptions of her life in France and Scotland. Consider the guidance you intend to give pupils; if the answers to any of the following questions are 'no' you may wish to revise your plans for guidance. If you cannot revise your plans sufficiently you may wish to return to 1a.
(i) Is the object of the work, as opposed to its subject, sufficiently clear to candidates?
(ii) If you are expecting lists of sources and references have candidates been told to provide them, and how to provide them?
(iii) Is the work going to be introduced in a lesson? If so how will you avoid candidates who miss the lesson being disadvantaged?
(iv) Will disadvantages to candidates joining the school after the work has been started be kept to a minimum?
If you are satisfied with your answers go to 2l.

2l Is your coursework spread evenly throughout the course or will it concentrate on certain times?
If evenly go to 3a. If concentrating on certain times go to 2m.

2m Possible overloading of candidates with coursework for various subjects due in at the same time in the school year is a major hazard. For example candidates might be expected to produce a major piece of coursework at the end of the fourth term in English, History, CDT, Geography, and Social Studies.

If your answer to many of the following questions is 'no' you might want to reconsider your answer to 1a.

(i) Do you have anything other than final deadlines for work to be handed in?

(ii) Have you a system to ensure that work is progressing during the timespan allowed rather than all being done in a rush at the end?

(iii) Will you allow any lesson time when coursework may be done?

(iv) Have you liaised with other departments about possible clashes of deadlines?

If you are satisfied with your answer go to 3a.

3 MARKING

3a What objectives are you required to provide marks for? Is there a regulation covering the breakdown of marks between objectives? If the work assesses more than one objective do you know how many marks you will allow for each objective?
When you are satisfied with your answer go to 3b.

3b Are you happy that you will be awarding marks only on the candidates' ability to meet the specified objectives?
When you are satisfied with your answer go to 3c.

3c Are you happy that your marking arrangements will distinguish between candidates on the basis of their positive achievement?
When you are satisfied with your answer go to 3d.

3d Are you happy that standards between various teaching groups will be exactly the same?
When you are satisfied with your answer go to 3e.

3e Are you happy that you will be able to show the moderator the thinking behind your award of marks?
When you are satisfied with your answer go to 4a.

4 ORGANISATIONAL CONSIDERATIONS

4a Answer the following questions about your scheme.
(i) How many assignments are you required to submit for moderation?
(ii) How many assignments will your candidates do?
Would your candidates benefit from doing more than the minimum number of assignments?
When you are satisfied with your answer to go 4b.

4b Will you record marks by assignment or by objective?
Go to 4c.

4c Will your record-keeping show up candidates with missing work in time to put the problem right?
If you are not satisfied with your answer reconsider 4b.
When you are satisfied with your answer go to 4d.

4d Will your record keeping show up weaknesses in the understanding of any particular objective by a group so that action may be taken? If you are not satisfied with your answer reconsider 4b.
When you are satisfied with your answer go to 4e.

4e Will occasional absence by pupils make it hard for them to have a complete set of coursework assignments?
If so reconsider your answers to 4a and 4b.
If you are satisfied with your answer go to 4f.

4f Will assignments usually be completed in class or for homework?
Go to 4g.

4g Are you happy that pupils' home background will not unduly hinder their chances of performing to their full potential?
If so go to 4h.
If you are not happy about this reconsider your answer to 4f.

4h Are you sure that the work you mark will be the unaided work of the candidate?
If you are not satisfied with your answer reconsider 4f.
If you are satisfied with your answer go to 4i.

4i Are you going to store candidates' work by assignment, or by candidate?
Will your solution be most useful to you during the course?
Will your solution help cut down on work when sending work for moderation?

Appendix B Examining groups for GCSE

London and East Anglian Group (LEAG)

East Anglian Examinations Board
The Lindens
Lexden Road
Colchester CO3 3RL
(Tel. 0206 549595)

London Regional Examining Board
Lyon House, 104 Wandsworth High Street
London SW18 4LF
(Tel. 01 870 2144)

University of London School Examinations Board
Stewart House
32 Russell Square
London WC1B 5DP
(Tel. 01 636 8000)

Midland Examining Group (MEG)

East Midland Regional Examinations Board
Robins Wood House
Robins Wood Road
Aspley
Nottingham NG8 3NR
(Tel. 0602 296021)

Oxford and Cambridge Schools Examinations Board
10 Trumpington Street
Cambridge CB2 1QB
(Tel. 0223 64326)

Oxford and Cambridge Schools Examinations Board
Elsfield Way
Oxford OX2 8EP
(Tel. 0865 54421)

Southern Universities Joint Board
Cotham Road
Cotham
Bristol BS6 6DD
(Tel. 0272 736042)

The West Midlands Examinations Board
Norfolk House
Smallbrook Queensway
Birmingham B5 4NJ
(Tel. 021 643 2081)

University of Cambridge Local Examinations Syndicate
Syndicate Buildings
1 Hills Road
Cambridge CB1 2EU
(Tel. 0223 61111)

Northern Examining Association (NEA)

Associated Lancashire Schools Examining Board
12 Harter Street
Manchester M1 6HL
(Tel. 061 228 0084)

Joint Matriculation Board
Manchester M15 6EU
(Tel. 061 273 2565)

Northern Regional Examinations Board
Wheatfield Road
Westerhope
Newcastle upon Tyne NE5 5JZ
(Tel. 091 286 2711)

North West Regional Examinations Board
Orbit House
Albert Street
Eccles
Manchester M30 0WL
(Tel. 061 788 9521)

Yorkshire and Humberside Regional Examinations Board
31–33 Springfield Avenue
Harrogate
North Yorkshire HG1 2HW
(Tel. 0423 66991)

Yorkshire and Humberside Regional Examinations Board
Scarsdale House
136 Derbyshire Lane
Sheffield S8 8SE
(Tel. 0742 557436)

Northern Ireland Schools Examinations Council (NISEC)

Northern Ireland Schools Examinations Council
Beechill House
42 Beechill Road
Belfast BT8 4RS
(Tel. 0232 704666)

Southern Examining Group (SEG)

Associated Examining Board
Stag Hill House
Guildford
Surrey GU2 5XJ
(Tel. 0483 506506)

South East Regional Examinations Board
2–10 Mount Ephraim Road
Tunbridge Wells
Kent TN1 1EU
(Tel. 0892 35311/2/3/4)

Southern Regional Examinations Board
Eastleigh House
Market Street
Eastleigh SO5 4SW
(Tel. 0703 664811)

The South Western Examinations Board
23–29 Marsh Street
Bristol BS1 4BP
(Tel. 0272 273434)

University of Oxford Delegacy of Local Examinations
Ewert Place
Banbury Road
Summertown
Oxford OX2 7BZ
(Tel. 0865 54291)

Welsh Joint Education Committee (WJEC)

Welsh Joint Education Committee
245 Western Avenue
Cardiff CF5 2YX
(Tel. 0222 561231)

Selected Bibliography

Batho, Gordon, Booth, Martin and Brown, Richard (1986) *Teaching GCSE History*, Historial Association pamphlet, looks at the origins and structure of GCSE, grade criteria and teaching strategies, assessment, coursework and the syllabuses available.

DES (1985) *History in the Primary and Secondary Years: An HMI View*, HMSO, encourages a skills and concepts basis for history teaching. Contains a useful matrix of skills and concepts with levels of understanding which pupils of given ages might be expected to achieve.

Dickinson A K and Lee P J (eds) (1979) *History Teaching and Historical Understanding*, Heinemann Educational Books, a collection of essays on recent innovations in history teaching. Subjects include educational objectives, curriculum projects, language and history teaching, children's thinking, examinations.

Dickinson A K, Lee P J and Rogers P J (eds) (1984) *Learning History*, Heinemann Educational Books, the follow-up to the 1978 volume. The essays focus on the ways in which pupils learn history. There are chapters on empathy and imagination in history, how pupils make sense of the past and assessment.

Fines, John (1984) *Source Based Questions at GCE A Level*, Historical Association pamphlet, TH 54, full of interesting material and examples which, though concerned primarily with the advanced level candidate, will be of use to the GCSE history teacher.

Historical Association, *Teaching History*, a journal published three times a year by the Association and available from them at 59a Kennington Park Road, London SE11 4JH. The journal, which was started in May 1969, is full of practical articles by practising teachers. Many of the articles are of direct relevance to the issues raised in this book.

Portal, Christopher (ed) (1987) *The History Curriculum for Teachers*, The Falmer Press, addresses a range of current issues in relation to the history curriculum in secondary schools.

Radio History, *GCSE History*, pamphlet accompanying two programmes broadcast 12–13 June, 1986 on Radio 4, and available from John Robottom, BBC Broadcasting Centre, Pebble Mill Road, Birmingham B5 7QQ. Cassette of programmes from BBC Emergency Cassette Service, Centre for Educational Technology, Civic Centre, Mold, Clwyd CH7 1YA. The programmes were based on work being done in schools. The booklet contains some of the teaching materials the pupils were using. Programme 1 looks at the use of historical source material; programme 2 at the teaching of concepts, empathy and coursework.

Rogers, Peter (1979) *The New History: Theory into Practice*, Historical Association pamphlet, TH 44, advances a rationale for the 'new history'.

Schools Council History team (1976) *History 13–16. A New Look at History*, Holmes McDougall, a useful summary of the Schools Council Project's philosophy, syllabus and assessment techniques.

Secondary Examinations Council in collaboration with the Open University (1986) *History GCSE. A Guide for Teachers*, Open University Press, describes the novel features of the GCSE examination. Sets activities which should prompt discussion of the new examining techniques and teaching approaches.

Shemilt, Denis (1980) *History 13–16: Evaluation Study*, Holmes McDougall, provides evidence that Project pupils can think historically at a more sophisticated level than pupils taught in a traditional manner.

Southern Regional Examinations Board (1980) *Explorations in Teaching Schools Council Project, History 13–16*, SREB, Eastleigh House, Market Street, Eastleigh, SO5 4SW, a wide-ranging collection of materials relating to the philosophy and teaching of the Project. Full of practical teaching and assessment suggestions. The materials are contained in a ring binder and have been updated twice.

Southern Regional Examinations Board (1986) *Empathy in History. From Definition to Assessment*, SREB, a practical booklet compiled by a group of teachers, examiners and lecturers.

Southern Regions Examinations Board (1987) *Use of Sources in History*, SREB, further volume from the same working party.